Library of
Davidson College

By the same author

The Aesthetics of Modernism
Anthology of French Poetry
Art and Knowledge
Britain and France, the Unruly Twins
Columbus's Isle
Contemporary French Poetry
Corsica, the Scented Isle
The Eagle of Prometheus *(poems)*
T.S. Eliot, Poet and Dramatist
France and the War
France and the Problems of Peace
The French Contemporary Theatre
Impressions of People and Literature
Landmarks of Contemporary Drama
Lights in the Distance *(poems)*
Mary Stuart *(verse play)*
The Necessity of Being
Paradoxes *(poems)*
The Poetic Drama of Paul Claudel
Realism and Imagination
Reflections on Life and Death
Reflections on the Theatre *(translation)*
Religion and Modern Society
Symbolisme — from Poe to Mallarmé
The Time of the Rising Sea *(poems)*
Twentieth-Century French Thought
White Temple by the Sea *(poems)*

Photo: Alfieri, Cannes, 1975

Collected
POEMS

JOSEPH CHIARI

with a preface by
Hugh MacDiarmid

NEW YORK
GORDIAN PRESS
1978

First published in the United States of America
in 1978 by the Gordian Press Inc.

© Joseph Chiari 1978
Preface © 1978 by C. M. Grieve

Library of Congress Cataloging in Publication Data

Chiari, Joseph.
Collected Poems.

I. Title.
PR9105.9.C5A17 1978   821   77-26826
ISBN 0-87752-213-8

Printed and made in Great Britain by
Skelton's Press, Cannon Place, Wellingborough,
Northants

PREFACE

I regarded it as a very great compliment when Jo Chiari asked me to write a short introduction to his collected poems, and while I did not feel qualified to do so, I agreed to do my best. I was therefore bitterly disappointed when I was unable to do so owing to a sequence of hospitalisations and operations. This brief preface is all I can manage in lieu of that absent introduction.

I have known Chiari for over thirty years. He was Cultural Attaché to the French Consulate in Edinburgh where he was exceptionally popular and helpful, and the memory of his genial personality is still treasured in the Scottish capital by all who knew him.

We had — and still have — many friends in common. Chief among them was T.S. Eliot whose work, like Chiari's, is in many ways at the opposite pole from my own. Both are learned poets, versed in several languages and literatures. Chiari is however predominantly a poet of Nature, but it would be even truer to call him a Natural Poet.

The poems assembled here exemplify that, but it is not nature in the raw he celebrates. It is nature mediated through a very vital personality of a profoundly philosophical disposition. His intellectual interests are not obtruded, however. These are reserved for his many prose books. It has been said that Dr. Chiari, author of *Aesthetics of Modernism, Realism and Imagination, Symbolisme — from Poe to Mallarmé,* and *The Necessity of Being,* "explores the intimate links between artistic creation and philosophical thought, and seeks to show how each strives to grasp the substance of human reality." This was said of his latest book, *Art and Knowledge* (Gordian Press 1977) — a very wise, profound, and beautifully expressed study which should be read by all interested in poetry today.

Even so, valuable as it is, that book, and all his other prose books, are but the *bagasse*. The wine is in his poems. I have enjoyed them and hope they will be appreciated by a wide public.

Hugh MacDiarmid

AUTHOR'S NOTE

This collection of poems is drawn from five previously published volumes. The first, *White Temple by the Sea,* was itself a selection made and presented by Edwin Muir, and has been compressed to one third of its original size which was over 150 pages. *The Eagle of Prometheus* has been reduced to two thirds of its size; *Paradoxes* has been left practically as it was. *Lights in the Distance* and *The Time of the Rising Sea* have each been reduced by a quarter. There are, at the end of this collection, a few poems which have not been previously published.

Corsican born, Corsican was my first language, French my second, English my third, and English is, like Corsican, a stressed, quantitative language. I was, very early in life, attracted to it and to its literature, and when I went to Scotland for post-graduate studies, I found there a spiritual home, and the English language became my natural medium of creative expression. Poetry is essentially rhythm and language as self-creating and continuously radiating experience, accessible to all those who wish to share it.

My friendship with Hugh MacDiarmid began soon after my arrival in Scotland, and nothing pleases me more than to have these collected poems, many of them written in Scotland, associated with the name of my old friend and Scotland's foremost poet.

To Joy

CONTENTS

From *White Temple by the Sea*, 1950
    Voyage   1
    White Temple by the Sea   2
    Eurydice   5
    Mediterranean Twilight   6
    Presence   7
    Lasting Frost   7
    Dawn   8
    Midges   8
    Lady with a Mirror   9
    The Graves   10
    The Far North   12
    Ulysses   13
    Remembrance   13
    In a Churchyard   14
    Life   16
    Night   17
    Spring Music   18
    Patience   18
    Memories   20
    Train   22
    Labyrinth   23
    Webs of Memory   24
    Light   28
    The Ever-Set Stage   30
    Oh! to Know   33
    Orpheus and Eurydice   34
    Prometheus   35
    My Words   36
    You and I   36
    White Sails   37
    Whither my Thoughts?   38
    My Heart   38
    The Heart and the Soul   39
    For You   40

Why? 40
Death of Hope 41
Night Journey 42
The Narcissus Girl 42
The Moon 43
Woman 44
Return 45

From *The Eagle of Prometheus,* 1953
Autumn Leaves 46
Poem 49
Enigma 50
Mist 51
Journey under the Sea 52
The Unfaithful 56
Let there be Peace 57
Marble-Dream 58
Spring 59
St. Peter's Sword 60
Graveyard by the Sea 62
Destiny 64
Procession 65
If I were not Sure 70
Trying to Write 70
Flight of a Bird 71
Dark of Night 71
Lovers' Talk 72
Tell Me 73
Into Your Hands 74
Parting 74
Without You 75
My Heart 76
Your Gifts 77
Lazarus' Lament 78
Pelican and Toreador 88
The Eagle of Prometheus 91

From *Paradoxes,* 1962
- Strange Woman   92
- When you Walk   93
- Language   94
- Forsake   94
- You Move Away   95
- Night   95
- The Order of Things   96
- Why Should You?   97
- Memory   98
- Lion and Unicorn   98
- Love   100
- The Cruel Town   100
- When I am Gone   101
- Our Logics are Different   103
- You will only Be   104
- The Heart   105
- Spring   106
- Prayer   107
- It's Time   108
- Dream   109
- They Say   110
- The Wisdom of Lime   111
- Autumn   111
- Home   112
- Strange Meeting   112
- To a Grounded Sailor   113
- Pieta   114
- Christmas Day   115
- Mazeppa's Ride   116
- Prayer   117
- Answer   117
- Lazarus   118
- What Matters   119
- In Mid Air   120

Three Songs:
  Gentle Boat   120
  Once I loved   121
  Waiting   121
To a Child Asleep   122

From *Lights in the Distance,* 1971
  Dancers' Dream   123
  Island-Born   123
  Deserted Village   125
  Filitosa   126
  Distant Valley   127
  Homeward   128
  Noon-Day Sun   128
  Asco   129
  Corsica   130
  When Night Falls   131
  Spiders   132
  The Intruder   133
  Try as I May   134
  Wouldn't You   134
  Night   135
  A Silent Fire   136
  You Are Being Followed   136
  What's the Use?   137
  Why Are We Here?   138
  Not the Years   138
  All that We Are   139
  Grief   140
  I Cannot Compare You   141
  The Snowman   142
  A Walk in the Park   142
  Slanting Sun   143
  Sun and Sea   144
  Why?   145
  To T.S. Eliot   147
  Thoughts by T.S. Eliot's Grave   147
  For Margaret   149

From *The Time of the Rising Sea*, 1975
    The Time of the Rising Sea   150
    Florence   152
    Edinburgh   154
    A Crow and I   155
    A Tree   156
    How Can I?   156
    Time   157
    Eclipse   158
    Conversation   158
    A Voice   160
    Eve   161
    Mediterranean Evening   162
    The Sea   163
    Today   164
    The Sun   165
    Cannes — Evening   166
    Setting Sun   166
    Mountain Lakes   167
    Presence   167
    Woman Asleep   168
    Absence   168
    Woman from a Painting   169
    I Remember   169
    If One Day   170
    Memento Yeats   170
    Morning   171
    Wisdom is Waiting   172
    Penelope-Sea   173
    Why Should You?   174
    Violets and Poppies   175
    Dawn   176
    Sea and Earth   177

Recent Poems
    Scotland   178
    Light   179
    Clouds   179
    Like Music   180
    Questions   180
    Who Am I?   181
    Kew Gardens 1974   182
    Hospital   183
    Man   184
    Morning Walk   184

VOYAGE

Suspended in space and time
I listen to the throbbing of the train
Through distances,
Tearing apart the web of warmth
In which we lived,
On the steel wheels
Of sidereal spaces
Towards platforms and stations
Strewn with ghosts and obsessions.

I watch the trees racing past,
Towards you,
And the grass bent by the wind
Of your words,
Fleeting golden leaves
Over the seas, blue
Like eyes,
Weighing over me
With the weight of all those
Who died before Christ
Lifted the stone from His tomb.

The earth races
With the heart racing against the train
Carrying my earth,
Dragging the kite of my thoughts,
Hovering over the grass where you lie
Or the grey stones where you live.

Sometimes I stretch my arm,
Through the shifting frame
Of the swift changing picture,
And brushing aside mountains,
Bending trees like blades of grass,

I find again the warm touch of your hand,
Then the world is golden
And soft as a peach
In an eternal Summer.

WHITE TEMPLE BY THE SEA

The sea laden with the unquenched tenderness
Of all those who found their last sleep
In her restless cradle,
Like an infinite hand with countless fingers
Caresses the red rocks lying at my feet,
And whispers of eternity to man's ephemeral fate.
White foam fringes the blue with gentle lace,
Which at times the wind lifts like a veil
Specked with shimmering diamonds.

A white marble temple displays the grace
Of its columns surging towards the tilted cup
Which stops their skyward growth.
The circling, gyring volutes
Remind me of my thoughts,
Without beginning or end.
Each day for years, in their intricacy,
I followed my dreams,
Changing, moving, regretting the dusk
That each night came shading the scene
Stretching in front of my eyes.
Dawn brought new hopes,
Never fulfilled,
Yet never killed
By falling night
Containing already the promises
Of the following dawn.

Birds, swift as arrows,
Dart towards the sea
To rise again, making in the sky
Patterns of lines, intricate,
Which like the lives of human beings never meet
In happiness,
For both are purely imaginary
And the best designs are those made by birds
Flying alone and not in pairs.

In my little temple by the blue sea
I met all the dwellers of my dreams.
White sails took me to shores
Where fair Iseult
Gave me the enchanted philtre
Which like the waters of Lethe
Left in my soul a void
Soon filled by her image.
With that image I lived, I walked,
I loved its shadow in which I found the source
Of a happiness the real world
Could never hold.
When that image disappeared
Others took its place,
Images of purity, of suffering without solace,
That of Mary, Clarissa or Heloise,
Of women of fame whose fate
And undying beauty
Have always moved the hearts of men.

The sun which every day shone
Over the white temple,
Spun webs of happiness unknown,
Unreal and yet understandable,
For those who remember
That Dante and Beatrice
Only met in Paradise.

But the sun sets or shelters in the shade of clouds,
Temples can be built or destroyed
By the hand of man
Or the hammer of time,
And dust, decay and ruins
Take the place of what was once
Beauty in praise of the Divine.

Happy he who like Ulysses,
After his voyages across the waves,
Returns home with renewed knowledge
And wisdom transcending the ages.

Absence is often met by a vacuum,
An empty seat round the table or fire,
An empty space where lay the house of our desires,
And ivy and broken columns
Where once stood grace and harmony
To fill the human heart with joy.

Such was the scene that met my eyes,
When after a night as long as years,
I returned to the shores
Where the white doves of my thoughts
Had for years found their nest.
I sat down on the ruins by the sea,
Looking at the dark narrow passage
Which separated the land
From the land on the other side,
I thought of that cold narrow passage
Which separates the world
From the world on the other side.
Night was falling,
Shadows were spreading their wings,
And looking over the other side of the land,

I could see in the thickening darkness
A cloud, a white speck,
White as a wedding veil,
The bridal veil of the unfailing guest,
The shroud that whitens all hopes.

EURYDICE

The dreams of a face
That one wants to see,
The sound of words
That one wants to hear,
Nail our thoughts
To the impatient heart,
Which, once satisfied,
Is like a desert after a mirage,
Crushed by the arid silence
That follows the word.

The word, like Orpheus' kiss,
Sometimes kills,
The image burns,
Silence is like Spring,
Absence is the night
Waiting for dawn,
Stretching its soft sinister wings;
So let us pray for the silence of Spring,
Let us hope for the permanence of night.

MEDITERRANEAN TWILIGHT

The sea, steel-blue blade,
Slides slowly
Above the golden head
Of the fallen God.

The air is crushed with silence,
Leaden like the rocks, barren
Myriads of years ago
When the warmth of the earth
Withdrew to the heart,
Waiting for the coming birth.

A last desperate beam,
A drowning hand,
Clings to the mountain's head,
And lingers dying
Over the sharp leaves
Of the dark green trees
Before the sky falls
Upon the waves,
With the last breath
Of the silent earth.

Standing on the shivering sand
I can feel the approaching weight
Of tidal sleep,
And I can hear silent worms
Creeping under my feet,
And the dust of bones
Falling towards the fire, where Time
Blends them anew into blood and stone.

PRESENCE

Your words like a hurricane wring my heart,
Your cold, lifeless grace
Burns my hands when in the depth of night
I shape the loved lines of your face.

When I paint the red curves of your lips against the dark,
I think that the wind of Lear will sweep my mind
Towards the dawn, grey like eyes, far away
Into the night of tomorrow, unborn, infinite
Like your promises.

Yet morning comes, with it comes my pain,
Your presence,
And wandering seaweeds tossed from ocean to ocean,
Have a less barren and restless existence,
Than a human heart caught in the tide of passion.

LASTING FROST

Snowdrops, heralds of cruel contrasts,
Break slowly under the winter frost;
Shall I ever feel the warm spring's fragrance
Break the frozen ice of your reticence?

Oh! the sadness of forgotten gardens
Filled with solitary, unattended flowers,
And the pathos of a bird singing a song
Which no companion ever answers!

DAWN

Dawn breaks at my window,
I lie weighing the silent minutes,
Thinking of you,
Thinking that your innocence and simplicity
Have been the Ariadne thread to the labyrinth heart.

At church I pray God and the saints, to purify my soul;
In vain; the only word which comes to mind
Is your name,
The only image which recurs, obsessing, overwhelming all,
Is that of your eyes, pale blue sea where I sail
My dreams,
And your soft scented hair is the dark forest
That ever throws my world out of its course.

Then Summer runs in my veins
And the thought of your glowing lips
Weighs upon my mind
Like a warm day in June.

MIDGES

Do your remember the road
Between the trees, marked blue,
And the twinge of the heart
At the thought
That soon we had to part?

Do you remember the dead wood
On which we sat,
The silence understood,
The words unsaid?

Do you remember the dark waters
And the midges,
Biting, piercing, like the obsession
Of our swelling desire
Beating against the ridges
Of our resolutions and conventions?

And last, do you remember the gate,
The parting kiss
And the wooden bars separating us,
Like Fate
That gives us the eyes
And the vision,
But never the guiding thread
And the means
To make of man's best dreams
Something more than illusions?

LADY WITH A MIRROR

My love, remember that gods and goddesses are dead
And lie buried under the hills
Or along the roads, in the groves
Where once they laughed and played.

Remember that your tender smile, your caressing eyes
And your statue-like features,
Reflected in a mirror, can only have the purity,
And also the aridity, of your desires.

Above all, remember
That whether you search for your Self
In your heart,
Or admire the changing shape of your face
In the reflecting glass,

There are never more than two eyes,
There is never more than one heart,
And your Self and the image reflected
Are like your shadow, which you can see
But cannot grasp or feel,
And which darkness always kills.

The earth made the body,
God made the soul, immaterial,
Universal, yet tied to decay,
Caught between darkness and light.

Mirrors, ice-needle waters,
Faithful reflections of your frozen grace
And illusions!
— The only mirror for the human soul
Is that of another soul,
Frail, broken by ripples,
Which at times make the image
Distorted, uncertain —
But they are the same ripples
That run in your perennial veins.

THE GRAVES

In days past, yet living with memories,
When our minds were swept by conflicting waves,
My love and I went home by the longest ways,
Through the cemetery along the graves.

And there the flowers,
The voices of the dead,
Spoke to us and said:
"Your lives are measured,
Your days are counted;
Your glowing eyes and living breath
Carry already with them
The cold mystery of death;
And through the roof of your promises
Roars the wind of frozen seas.

Why then wait, why waste
Precious moments while death hastes?
Why torment, even for a fleeting minute,
Your frail hearts
Which soon will cease to beat?
Why fail to realise
That death is a constant weight,
Which only love and faith
Can for a moment lift?"

And these wordless whispers,
These stares from empty sockets,
And the sound of bones striking relentless hours
Made us feel that our light would soon darken,
While grass and trees would continue to dress
Alternately in brown or green,
And that unmoved by our disappearance,
Birds would continue to sing
And roses would maintain their fragrance.

And, like Prometheus sheltering his new discovery
From the rising winds,
We left that mirror of life, that cemetery,
Cupping in our hands the flame
Of our reborn promises.

THE FAR NORTH: Sutherland

This is the end of the earth,
And the hills, tired and worn out,
Crouch in despair and brood,
By the side of roads
As straight as boredom.

Here the loom of life
Hardly moves,
And the breath which heaves
The trunk of the earth
In a mighty strife
Up to the clouds,
Hardly stirs these extremities.

Here time has no meaning,
And the sound of boots
Breaks the silence of bare feet
Treading the roads
That throughout the ages
They have traced.

Here the human voice
Has preserved the raucous tones
Of time when thought
Lay asleep in the womb
Of the inchoate word,
When the sun and the seasons
And man's fears and his urges
Rhythmed the pulse of life,
And when man and woman
Could, in the fading light,
Contemplate their image — one
In the waters —
And, with the song of the lark,
Open to the world their eyes
That had never seen the flood and the ark.

ULYSSES
To M.

Shrieks of wheels, throbbing of engines,
Space widens between you and me tonight,
Yet I can feel your face and above the noise of machines
I hear music, and under my eyelids I can see the light.

Calypso and her charms,
Circe and her magic
Could never allay Ulysses' qualms
And make him forget the shores of Ithaca.

Wayward as Ulysses, perhaps, yet not so,
Dreaming of the seas, sailing the clouds,
Minerva steering my ship past the islands,
Making for home towards your weaving hands.

Happy as Ulysses to find the ever-burning flame,
Happier than Ulysses for having been spared
The weight of roaming years and the nymphs of fame
Who ensnared his soul and delayed his journey home.

REMEMBRANCE

If only we could remember
The red,
Not the red of the roses
Or the red of the robes,
But the red of the dead,
And the birth in December;

If only we could remember
The pledges born and dead
Like flowers of lasting red,
And the words which, in the April night
And the recurring rains, remained
Unanswered;

If only we could remember,
Not the bugles, the flags and the speeches,
But the loves and the wishes
Of those who were made heroes
But would have preferred
The living flame to the embers;

If only we could shed bitter tears
and not pious words and holy water
On dead stones with dark names,
Then perhaps our memories
Would give birth to flames
More stirring than a yearly prayer.

IN A CHURCHYARD

Here lies,
But does not rest,
One who believed
While he lived
That under the grass
Or the dead leaves
Peace would come at last.

Here lie side by side
Those who loved
And did not love,
Those who hated
And inflicted pain,
And those who waited
For Spring in vain.

All of them thought
That there was a birth and a death,
That when their eyes were shut
And their hearts had ceased to beat,
The waves that swept their veins
And the thorns that pierced their minds
Would never more be felt.

Oh! the desert of the flesh
Which never felt the rain,
And of the heart
Which never felt the light!
But oh! the desert of dusts —
Essences of longing —
Lying side by side,
Waiting without hope
Through endless night
And with serpents — sorrows —
Clasping their immovable shadows.

Oh! the sun-devouring pain
Of the golden dust of Helen,
Ground throughout the infinite day
By the merciless light
Dispelling the Lethean night,
Without any hope of return
To the Trojan shores
And the warmth of the face

Or the veil of the eyes,
To hide from Menelaus
The ever piercing lies!

High mountains will end in sands,
Huge forests in the womb of the earth,
And the undying essences
Will assume the countless shapes
Of tormented trees,
Suffering animals or men,
Yet each one will retain its fixed fate,
Of lasting love
And lasting hate,
Until Time's last breath.

LIFE

We live surrounded by appearances;
We do not feel the waves
Creeping under the sands,
Or the gnawing worm
Which beyond blossom
And green leaves,
Reduces fibres to dust
And new dawns
In shifting winds.
We live waiting for tomorrow,
Waiting for time.
Are we time, a departure,
An arrival never reached,
A race by the heart-clock, and the stars
Which follow us
Round the bends of minutes,

Pursuing a future
Which is our past
Ever-present, ever recast
Along the roads of time,
Without beginning or accidents,
And where only death
Dies with us to be born again?

NIGHT

The light fades,
The day lays its sleepy head
On stones at street-corners,
On thorny couches
In shrubby rooms.

Night unlocks pains
And hopes which light
Had kept hidden,
And across the stage
Of weary minds
Rush the gnomes and demons
Which were afraid of the sun.

Sleep lies in chains,
Waiting for Death to free him,
And the heart and the mind
Are a garden fete
Or a battlefield
Streaked with a thousand fires.

At last, pale dawn softly creeps
Amongst faded petals
And forlorn remains,
Across frozen fields
Where, merciless, rises
The self-devouring Self.

SPRING MUSIC

Joyful trees reel up the hill,
A spring shyly peers through the wood
And returns to its frightened hole.
Birds from all corners of the earth
Flock more numerous
Than leaves can shelter.

The spring reappears in the tempting sun,
Eurydice leans thoughtfully
Against a golden stem
Waiting for the music
And for the birds to sing to her
The songs that she wants to hear.

She waited for many tides
And winds,
Many cycles of the moon,
Until on a hollow night
The hill swallowed the trees
And the birds like dead leaves.
Then the spring returned to earth,
And Eurydice to the underworld
And to the flowers,
Which she had failed to gather.

PATIENCE

Patience, patience across this sea of waste
Whence each day surges a new wreckage,
Patience, patience when the heart
Throbs on to its end like a ghost train
Racing through dark woods and deserts
Towards the waiting chasm!

Wait, wait, constantly reminded
Of the scent of the open earth
And the approaching winds
Of the last judgment!
Stand still, like the magnetic needle
Of an ever shifting pole,
Nailed by the piercing fear
Of eternal stillness!

Wait, stem the stream of life
Rushing like a torrent
From rock to rock
Down the mountain
To the depth of the ocean!
Wait, control the beats
Of the heart,
The lightning visions of the mind,
The mirages, the hallucinations
Of the tired eyes,
Wait for the breeze
That never rises,
And the fountain which never flows!

How I understand the melancholy of trees
Tied to the earth for centuries,
Woodenly faithful to their lovers,
Friends, neighbours or brothers,
Among stones whose silence
Is more moving than the strings
Of any violin.
I can often detect in the rustle
Of their leaves
The echo of my words,
Whispers of my thoughts,
And I think that once perhaps
In the haze of years

They were what I am,
And that they are now as I shall be,
Or will be, for aeons of years,
Those who could never stand with patience
On the dreaded ledge of silence,
And wait with steady faith
For the end and the beginning.

MEMORIES

I remember the womb of the waters
And the dust of the ages
Which still fills my scared eyes,
I remember the icy nights
Of the endless polar lights
And the burning breeze
Of the deserts where hot sands
Bleached white my bones.

I remember the steppes
And the stormy seas,
The holes where I crawled,
The protecting trees,
The shores dear to Minos
And the calm waters of the Piraeus.

I still hear Cassandra's cries
On the crumbling walls of Troy,
And my blood is the driving force
Which gave life to the Pyramids.

I have been Prometheus
Nailed by the heart
On his rock of pains,
I remain Prometheus,
Feared by the gods,
Master of my pains;
With the torch of the heart
Lighting the earthly paths
Which fate wrapped in night.

I have been Christ with the aching heart,
Carrying the weight of a million years;
My shoulder still bleeds
With the wounds of the cross,
And from the depth of my mind ever rises
The horror of the betrayal,
The agony in the olive groves
And the memory of night
Stabbed by the shriek of the owl.

I remain Christ,
Dreaming of the heights
And unsolved mysteries;
I know the numbers
Which compose the harmonies
That guide the stars
Through the infinite spaces.

I make eternity
With my perennial bones,
I can hear the music
Of the earth,
And I can see the golden needle of light
Piercing through the vision
Of perfection,
Which will mark the death of Time
And the end of God's creation.

TRAIN

The train ploughs its way
Across the earth, dark or green,
Across fields, golden,
Past trees
Clinging with wistful fingers
To the windows
Beyond which I sit,
Listening to the throbs of the wheels.

Sometimes the train disappears
Into the folds of the earth,
And the only thing the eyes can see
Is a ribbon of pale blue sky
Waved in the wind by an iron hand,

Sometimes it leaps over gaps
Across the wrinkles of its aged face,
Making frightened blades of grass
Shudder under its thundering weight;

Sometimes it slips into the land of dreams,
Racing past glades and streams,
Speaking words which no man every knew,
And which fade with the morning dew.

It visits the moon and the stars,
It races round galaxies and clouds —
The infinite veils of the skies,
In which the earth lies lost
Like a ball fallen from a child's hands.

But whether I travel for hours
Or for years across space,
The end of the race
Always brings me
To the beginning of the journey,
To Solitude
Whence the train left.

LABYRINTH

Life is the Labyrinth
In which man cannot retrace
His steps or avoid the gate
Of the waiting precipice.

Like the ant he hastens,
Over stones
And road companions,
Falls or is trampled by them,
But can never pause
On his appointed race.

Lost in the maze of ways,
He never knows which path
Leads to the happy groves,
Where the scent of flowers
And the song of birds
Will make him forget
The gate where the coffin waits.

Like the ant, which never discovers
Until the winter
Whether it endured pains
To carry husks or grains,
He never knows until the last stage
Of his voyage
If the places that he liked
Or the decisions in which he believed
Were in the pattern of the eternal good
Or mere loved illusions.

It is only from the heights
That one can see the forest and its paths,
And man must wait
Until he has reached the end,
To decide at last, where he was right
And where he was lost.

WEBS OF MEMORY

To Pierre Emmanuel

Who am I? Who are you?
Whose face do I see,
Whose voice do I hear,
When Time fades and dies
In the Lethean blue
Of your elemental eyes?

Swells of words seem to surge
From the age-old sea
To your prehistoric lips,
Eyes infinite like the skies
Illumine the ages,
And from the diamond sun
Pours down the flame
That flows in the veins of the earth
Along the fibres of trees,
The wings of birds,
And through the tenuous filaments
Of the perennial flowers.

Myriads of hands,
Webs of memories,
Spring from the living earth
To mould the shapes
Born from the boundless void,
Reflecting in their primal form
The colours of the eternal sea,
And sounds as old as the skies.

Are the words that I hear
When you speak
Copt, Hebrew or Greek?
Do they come to ears

Which have already
Heard those sounds,
And is it the warmth
Of the Egyptian sands
That burns the palm
Of your hands?

Who am I? Who are we?
Harlequins, kings or beggars,
Trees, stones or flowers,
Particles of an ever-changing whole,
Aeolian harps singing
With the winds of the ages,
Masks of countless shapes
Treading the mysterious roads
Of man's progression
From Eternity to Eternity!
Memories of icy nights
When the sun was lost,
Dreams of oases —
Silver and green specks
On burning sands —
Hallucinations of the steppes
Or of the seas,
Which still lull our bodies,
Murmurs of the Nile
And of the Euphrates,
Or whispers of mysterious hours
Spent on shores where the mist
Turns sea-weeds
Into long flowing hairs,
And the music of the wind
Into inviting songs!
Yesterdays and tomorrows
But never today,
Echoes of voices or glimmers

Of chaos reflecting the future,
Already made, yet unseen
By human eyes, unheard
By human ears,
But as present in the folds
Of the unfolding years
As image and event
Already exist in the shafts of light
That stream from their projector source
Onto the screen of the earth
Or onto the walls of the brain.

The sun knows the span
Of its oscillations,
The stars the timelessness
Of their revolutions,
Each one knows the path
Of its celestial race,
Without beginning or end
Like the circle of the universe.

If you could stand at the source,
At the God-head of life,
You would see the primal needle of light
Travelling through infinite clouds
And starry spaces,
Broadening over aeons of years
Into the eyes, hands and faces
Which embrace the earth,
You would see neutrons and protons
Begetting the first atom,
Spawning in seas and lands
Vegetal and animal shapes,
You would see water flowing from burning stones,
Trees lifting their heads in the briny air,
Fishes silently invading the lands,

And stars lost in shifting sands,
You would meet songs looking for birds,
Eyes looking for human faces,
And affections as cold as ice
Looking for hearts to harbour them,
You would hear the echoes of names
Of past and coming fames,
And on the memory of timeless space
Which stores light and sounds,
You would see Christ's cross-shape
On the hill of Calvary,
And Socrates drinking the hemlock,
You would see dreams looking for heads,
Hopes for human hearts,
Lost words for friendly ears,
And the ark which, after the atomic flood,
The new Noah is going to lead,
You would hear man's words to the dinosaur
And the sound of Greek feet on Mount Athos.
If you had the eyes that could see,
You would watch the transformations
Of people and civilisations,
And you would see life
Unfolding on the screen of the earth
And lasting until its warmth
Fades and, worn-out,
It joins the moon on the scrap-heap
Of celestial remains.

Who made the film,
Whence does it come?
Seen from the supreme height,
The world gestates in the atom,
And the microcosmic ray of light
Born from the eternal eye
Broadens into universal life.

Men are only the particles
Which compose the shafts of light,
They think that their questions,
Hesitations and actions
Are self-willed and free,
And can alter the living stream;
Ever too close to the screen,
They can only see what lies
Under their eyes,
But never the whole picture
Of life, and its frame of nature,
For they can never rise and see
The all-embracing cone of light
From the distance and the height
Which fuse centuries into seconds,
And men and nations into the grains
Of the eternal sands.

LIGHT

Try with the eyes to encompass space
Or to pierce the immensity of the skies,
Try to fathom the depth of light
Which surrounds our night,
And, modern Icarus, you will soon lie
On the broken pieces of your glassy eye.

Watch the sun, broken wheel
Of the heavenly chariot,
Blazing endlessly across the sky,
Watch the earth, vestal of fate,
Salomé of the countless veils
Dancing round a king who ever maintains
The same distance,

Ask yourself where is the Charioteer,
Where is the king or the musician
Who knows the harmonies
Of the infinite spaces,
And you will be plunged into a fall,
Endless, down and down,
Towards the dark, towards places
Where lie wriggling, blind,
Writhing like sectioned serpents,
The broken numbers
And the shattered aberrations
Of Reason.

There you will understand
That you can never bring together
With your pygmy hands
The moon and the Pole star,
Orion and the Hunter,
And you will throw away into space
Your myopic spyglasses
With which you try to scan the universe,
And, your pride ground to dust,
You will shut your eyes,
And wait.

And from the centre of the earth
To the deserts of the moon,
From the golden rays of the sun
To stars lost in millions of years,
From the roots of restless trees
To the penitent stones of the roads,
From the seas of your birth
To the flame of your living death,
Countless hands will cling to yours
And lead you to the shores
Where eternity roars.

Pure crystal sea, whiter than the white,
Brighter than the light,
Dazzling point
In which lie drowned
The infinite universe
And the broken pieces of Time,
Bliss, where the light
Disappears into the glory of Light,
And the heart becomes the music
Of the silent harmonies, source
Of the everlasting prayer, fused
In the molten whiteness of Eternity!

THE EVER-SET STAGE

We think of trains running on rails,
Of rivers racing down mountains and plains
Towards the waiting sea, to begin again
The cycle of rising clouds and falling rain,

But we think of life as a firework in the sky,
An explosion in the night, a silver column
Of conflicting forces, past and present,
Spilling at random on tomorrow's void.

We moan, and repeat with recurrent regret
That had Cleopatra's nose been shorter,
The face of the world would have been different,
The earth would have been another planet.

We forget that Cleopatra could only be
With her nose, neither shorter nor longer,
But what it was already in the loins of creation,
What it had to be, since the birth of the sun.

The whole world, from the birth of light
To the last pangs of Christ, could not be altered
To make Mark Antony turn away unmoved
And indifferent to the sorrows of her defeat.

Napoleon could only be in 1789,
When the people of Paris were loading the guns;
And the wind which shook the European thrones
Was already at work in Adam's breath.

If we could reach the vertiginous height,
The height beyond space and distance,
The height whence surges infinite light,
We would see at a glance the whole web of life,

We would see on that shadowy veil
William Pitt on the banks of the Thames,
And Nelson's eagle eye spying the sails
With which he lit the torches of fame,

We would understand that in the maze of strands
Which weave the pattern of life,
The whole fabric would break
If each atom or thread could choose its own direction.

There has been a birth which contains its end,
The apple pip cannot bring forth a palm tree,
Through the seed the timeless eye can see the fruit,
There has been a separation, and Eternity waits.

Was Christ born from Mary and, the Crucifixion?
No, Christ was born, and crucified, with Creation,
He lives in every man, He dies in every man,
And every human action is His martyrdom or glory.

He lives in our hearts, gnawed by our sins,
He is Prometheus chained by man's lowest deeds,
We raise the knife, and His heart bleeds
With the blood which can wash all stains.

He fills our hearts with light and hope,
We are the spear which pierces His side,
And the living Cross upon which He lies,
Imploring us for His Redemption.

Yet, there was a birth two thousand years ago,
In God's time Christ-God took human shape
From the Virgin's womb and put on the shirt of sin
Which had weighed upon man since Adam;

His presence and His words became the symbols
Of Eternity which man could understand,
His longing for His Father, His sufferings
Through man's hands, are those of us all,

Chirst's humanity shows God's solidarity
With His creation — source of imperfection and pain,
It shows that Christ-God has consented to suffer
In body and spirit until the last resurrection.

We talk of Blake's visions and magic flights;
Did his starry eyes give life to the void,
Did he write or paint as if with Divine hands,
Could he, with his skill, shape nothingness?

No, what he saw and heard was as old as the world;
He merely remembered or recaptured sounds
And visions which had already struck other eyes,
Other ears — those of Dante, Milton and Plotinus.

Whispers and visitations from far-away worlds
Break, at times, through the veil of life;
Must we confuse the echo for the source,
The trembling of the veil for the living force?

Words, wings of infinite voyages,
Chains which tie man to earth,
Light by which he sees and knows
The wounds of time and the call of the womb,

Words cannot make anew; they only remind
Man of what, without eyes or ears,
He once lived in the whirling light
Where lay his form and that of creation.

OH! TO KNOW

Oh! To know the sounds and colours
That could suggest or unfold
The grey blue of the seas
And the russet gold
Of the autumn leaves!

To know how to steal
From silence
The words and the music
In which eternity lives!

To be able to discover the scent
And the song of the roses
Whose petals, stirred by the breeze,
Have the softness
Of haunting eyes!

To suspend time
In a word,
And hold the world
In my hand,
To lay it at your feet
With humility,
And disappear in your love,
Like a river in the sea!

These are the thoughts
Which, since Time and birth,
Have filled my memory.

ORPHEUS AND EURYDICE

Why should I steal her from Eternity
To bring her back to death?
Why should I be disturbed
By the grey seas of her pleading eyes
And the golden lava
Of her outstretched arms,
And tear her away from the unifying fire
Where forever she will lie?

Why give death with words,
When silence is life?
Ah! let her lie dead
In the infinity of possibilities,
Wrapped in the ethereal veils
Of tomorrow's promises,
As if all the stars of the skies
Had sheltered under eyelids
That will never be lifted!

Let her for ever be, nothing
And everything,
Let her burning heart
Have the stillness of stone,
Let me be drunk to madness
With what could have been,
And let me wait for the day
When my heart, overflowing with songs,
Will be torn to pieces,
Like a harp by the tempest
That it refuses to sing!

PROMETHEUS

Wrecked for all time on his rock,
Wracked by wailing winds and the seas,
Furrowing his hollow frame,
Filled with fire, there he lies;

There he lies, his red-gushing flesh
Endlessly pierced by the flint of the fall
From God's Heaven into the land
Where with his hands he made his son of God.

The wound is in the flesh, God created,
Gnawed by the memories of the fire — one,
Ever rising to the lost Heaven,
Ever tied to the earth — womb of the Word.

Love, knowledge of God,
Drove him to the earth and to the attempt
To bring to man the Pentecostal fire
And the faith which nailed him to the rock.

He might have remained a god or an angel
In the Elysian fields, in a place
Of transparency and divine bliss,
Timeless, though unknown without hell;

But love drove him to the knowledge of pain
And the descent into dark realms
Whence, with the red heart of man, he rises
Towards the still centre of eternal light.

MY WORDS

My words, expressions of pain,
Of wind and rain wrung by the storm,
In vain falling on fallow ground
Drier than any desert, barren,

My heart grieves, when the grey sky
Reflects your eyes, mysterious veils
Strewn with stars which strayed
From the Milky Way to dormant pools,

My green hands grow thorns when the shadow
Of your shape is all that remains
From the lethal weight of night journeys,
From the unrelieved darkness of endless days,

And the fever that burns your lips
Flows like white waves of flame
Round the island-heart and the flower,
And consumes both in the infinite fire.

YOU AND I

My selves live with the ghosts
Of the selves that I have lost,
My words surge from the books
That burn with Helen's looks,

My gardens of love are swept
By the wind of leaves
That sang in the olive groves
Or fell from northern trees,

My house is filled with strangers
Whom I meet on the doorsteps
Or on the stairs,
They nod and pass,
I stammer and stare,
Wondering who they are.

Some remember the veils
Of the seven dances,
Some dance them still,
I don't know who they are,
I don't know where you are.

If I take your hand for a walk
In the mountains,
You become the mountain,
And I walk through woods and vales
Until I reach the well
Of the never-told-tales.

WHITE SAILS

The life-awakened waves
Wound with their claws
The waiting shores,
Their age-long graves.

The fast-flying wind
Wails through the leaves of trees
The complaint of distant seas,
The agonies of Time's wound.

The earth stands still
And clouds grip the heart,
Freezing its furrowed vales,
While, silent, I wait
For the white sails.

WHITHER MY THOUGHTS?

Whither my thoughts, towards what islands,
What shelter or red-roofed houses
Will you stretch your wings
To follow your king of the grey seas?

Whither my eyes of the heavenly skies,
Haunted by yesterday's stars and lost boreal lights,
Will you bend the hopelessness
Of your broken flight?

Whither my heart, hollow shape,
Deserted as a haunted house,
Will you drag your stony weight,
But towards the waiting, maternal earth?

I, and never I, crossroad of many winds,
Solitary tree swarmed over with resting birds,
I dream, dumb, of my dead song,
I shudder, cold, at my lost leaves.

MY HEART

My heart, let the candle of sorrow
Die out in the wind which with time flows,
And let my shade cease to follow
The shifting selves of shadows.

Let my still blood forget the race
From restless limbs to age-old face,
Let the pangs and the pains die
At last, in the silence of sidereal tides.

Let me forget the song of birds,
The glimmer of gold in the immemorial night,
And the whispers of winds that I have felt
With the fallen leaves of lost loves.

My heart, cease to grieve for the dying,
And let the burrowed bones return
To the brine of the sea, more living
Than the whims of the wandering moon.

Let the grave be your comfort-room,
Deaf to the murmur of the waves
And to words woven on earthly looms
With the web of man's perennial grief.

THE HEART AND THE SOUL

Oh the torment of hours falling forlorn
On pastures bare, grazed by alien flocks,
While the hair grows grey and the eyes
Grow dim with the light of lost memories,

My heart waiting under the wrinkles,
Trembling for my soul buried along the banks
Of ancient rivers, gazing in waters
Reflecting the dust of rising stars,

My heart hollowed by the waves of Time,
Draining the blood to nameless depths,
Waiting for my soul to realise that tomorrow
Ever rises from the seas of the eternal past.

When, oh when will my soul cease to soar
Towards clouds white as night,
Searching for doves which have long died
And can never rise from today's waves?

WHY?

Why did I come to this town
Where I stand divided and torn
For having only once known
The cold wind of Heaven?

Had I not met you, I might have been
Another, that hollow self unseen,
A dream of Spring ever green,
Without you I might have been another.

And so I wait for the infinite sleep
Of your ocean eyes blue and deep,
And for the cold grave, the only place
Where I shall forget the weight of the ice
And the grief of your grey ghostly grace.

FOR YOU

For you, king of my dead nights,
I shall build a town of rags,
A town where the sun never rises,
Where darkness never ends,

A town with its walls in ruins,
With its houses stabbed with holes,
Letting through the wind and the rain
Like a heart pierced by pain.

Ghost of my dead nights
Haunting my ruins, I shall bury you
In a palace of graves,
In a sea of dreams rejecting you
Like the hollow hull of grief.

Presence of my white nights,
Obsessing ruler of my fallow frame,
I shall drown you in the flames
Of my burning town consumed white
By the grinning skeleton of Adam.

Then at last, dawn will come
And the sun will shine on lawns
Where, united with my King of Light,
I shall rise in the flames of His vision.

DEATH OF HOPE

There was a time when, nailed on my ruins,
I shuddered at the whispers of leaves,
And I burnt in the lightning of flames
Heaven-sent, laden with hopes and pains,

A time when my multitudinous selves
Were bleeding with the thorns of Heaven,
And when from the glimmers of a distant dawn
Rose the searing tongues of subterranean fires.

Now, Heaven can torment me no more,
For hope, Phoenix ever reborn from broken days,
Is dead, and, freed from its woes and power,
I roam unmoved along Hell's heavenly ways.

NIGHT JOURNEY

When at night I remain alone,
I walk along lime-scented lanes,
My head leaden with love
Longing to roll down to the depth of doom.

Then in my mind I crawl, with care and fear,
Along vales and hills where treasures dear
Lie hidden under dancing blood
And stars buried in sacred woods,

Palatial domes rise from leafy slopes,
The land of a thousand and one nights
Unfolds under my eyelids,
And time drowns in the wells where you lie.

After infinite journeys, round the planets
And the Milky Way, after having burnt
Bright in the blaze of the sun, I return
To the earth to sleep, the sleep of stones.

THE NARCISSUS GIRL

When the evening like a serpent creeps
Along the ripples of my loosened hair
And the still curves of my fallow hips,
Steel blue under the moon's sisterly stare,

I shudder under the weight of ice,
And my inward turned eyes
Transfix me to the earth with crystal spears
Of my beloved, frozen tears.

I love the horror of my net of robes
Sheltering the shivering marble
Of my sculptured arms and the graves
Of my moon-hollowed breast.

I long for the land of the virgin-ice
Reflecting the pure lines of my whiteness
Hallowed by fleeting clouds and stars,
Trembling under the weight of dreams.

Then I can feel the harmonies of my nudity,
Unstained by the solar heat of the serpent
Stranger, spreading its sinuous flesh
Across the silence of my self-frozen lakes.

THE MOON

Oh moon, wanderer of the night,
Frigid lover of immemorial seas,
What urge, what daemonic delight
Makes you give rise to ever-defeated tides?

Waves of white flames
Follow in the wake of your briny feet
Into the night, into the deep darkness
Of tides and passions spent.

Oh moon of my tidal days,
Restless source of my ebbs and flows,
What memories, what taboos
Wrap your face in steely veils?

Tell me, oh tell me what lies
In the hollow of your silvery eyes,
And what sombre scars or grace
Hide your unseen mysterious face?

Oh moon — Danae-like woman,
Blind vestal of tidal fires —
What fate, what sin of man
Entrusted you with spears and nails?

Oh when will my feeble flesh and the sea
Cease to be moved by your command,
And when will my tideless weeds
Be lulled to sleep by moonless winds?

WOMAN

Woman, mother-of-all, wound of all men,
Mysterious mediator of man's wintered soul,
Serpent of flames slowly searing the cells,
Born to burn for the return to the womb.

Woman, word of God written on random leaves,
Mother of God, the life-giving flame,
The grace which to Heaven heaves us,
The quick-silver which weighs in our veins.

Infinite web wrapping the world,
Weak without your azurean veil,
White without the blood-stained
Lips and the spear of Christ's wound.

Mother, the air we breathe,
The breeze which bathes our face,
The song which mellows the trees
Into words of immemorial warmth.

Lover, grave-digger of the heart,.
Grinding man on the stones of your hands
Until the gruelling grief of your flame
Consumes his soul into the call, for the Mother.

RETURN

The sun, sphere of fire, surges
From the blue of the slumbering sea;
In the sky the last star shimmers
And fades away in the rising dawn.

In this valley brimming with ghosts,
Like conflicting winds in the Aeolian cave,
My sun breathes an alien light, lost
In woods where nothingness lives.

My mind's shores are flooded
With countless weeds, floating past,
Tossed endlessly over the rocks
Where glimmers the ghost light
Of dreams drowned in night.

A bird's song, a tinkling bell,
Today and tomorrow, time dies
In the absence where I lie,
Staring at the sun which devours.

Do I race like the wind swallowing space,
Or do I stand still like the Pyramids,
Watching the Nile nibbling away their sandy feet,
Blind to the waves which furrow their fate?

Who knows, who will tell?

AUTUMN LEAVES

I

If there are moments when the sap slows
In the limbs, with the weight of winter,
When beads of frost slide down the bare wood,
When echoes of footsteps resound through the hollow
Heart, and memories stir dead roots,
It is now when leaves float in the air
And, tossed by the whims of winds, slowly fall
Down to earth.
This is the time when haunting shapes
Linger in the shaft of light
Left behind by the fast-fading sun;
It is the time when words lost in the scent of lime
Return with lips red as berries,
The time of distant gulls lacing rocks
Washed by the foam of endless waves,
Older than the marble where Venus sleeps,
Mysterious like the waters of mountain lakes,
The time when one walks into rooms crowded
With absent faces and faded memories,
The time when one leans through windows
Over the obsessing depths of the restless sea
Glittering dark between her lashes of leaves,
Watching the shadows which stain her face
And weigh more heavily on her bosom
Than all the boats which throughout the centuries
Have ploughed across her timeless waves.

II
What flame, what fire
Fuses thoughts into tears, fallen
Beads of regrets from burnt hours
And the embers of desire;
What urge compels my hands
To mould old marble,
My eyes to see loved lands,
And words to rise like doves
From ancient gables
At the crowing of dawn;
What force, friend or foe,
Invades the fortress of the heart
And breaks the smooth surface
Of the pond, which now reflects
Broken images and crumbling walls?
I know the force, I know the gate
Through which friends and foes walked in,
I know the hands and the light
Which in the night guided their steps.
Friends and foes, all in one, indefinable,
The return of all in the final act of the play,
The last gathering before the end;
Welcome friend, wanted foe,
More than friend, dream with whom
I have lived; how can I know
Which to trust, which to kill?
Yet one must die, that the other may live!

III
The years fall with the dying leaves
And winter, zenith of life, watches
From its still heart of revolving dust
A procession of white-robed monks —
Water-drops sliding along roads of wires

On a rainy day — trudging on, and on,
Towards what holy lands, what end, who knows?
Yet there they go, blindly, endlessly,
Like the multitudinous sons of Adam, walking
With heavy feet and bowed heads, tramping
For millions of years over mountains and steppes,
Across vast stretches of ice and tempest-tossed seas,
From the lost gates till the trumpet's sound
And the rising flames of the Last Judgment.
An apple tree bare in the winter light,
Stretching its beads of pearly hair,
Watches over them with that detachment
Which the sun, the moon and the perennial stars
Have forever cast over the laughter and tears,
The dreams and the nightmares of men.
And man will forever hope and fear
The scent of spring and the last flower,
The rise and fall of the leaves,
The cyclic tides of the seasons
And the patience of the waiting sands,
And like one of those fabulous animals,
Cast upon the dry sands of the oceans,
He watches with gasping breath
The moon hauling away the waves,
Knowing that soon he will be water
Rolling across silent seas,
Or dust or loam nursing in the earth
The seeds and forms of recurring births.
Oh the sadness of autumn leaves,
And the glow of St. Martin's Summer,
When fire and ice burn into living memories,
When the mellow sun of December
Turns to rosy wine the winter snow,
And when the fumes of this dreamt-of liquor
Make, for one moment, the heart forget
The weight of the years

And the wisdom of the head!
Oh piteous heart, bend,
Break now, bury your head
Into the ashes of the remaining hours,
And shudder at the ice
Of seeing, at last, Love
Face to face!

POEM

To walk across the streets entranced,
Unaware of the wind and the grimy stones,
Feeling nothing but the force
Of your eyes and the dream of things undone,

To see in every shape of trees
The curve of your restless arms,
And beyond the brown fog, to descry
The golden lights of mountain lakes,

To transform hail and rain
Into the redness of your glowing lips,
And to feel in the wind the endless web
Of your sun-scented hair,

Such is the fate which since the joy of dawn
Has been, and will forever be, mine.

ENIGMA

In what century
Have I seen you,
On what golden sands
Did the blue of night
Wrap my mind as in a net
Held by a thousand hands?

Was it on the banks of the Nile
By the statue of Isis,
That in my dreams I sailed
The obsessing seas of your eyes?

Was it before the flood
When man, animals and birds
Spoke the same language
That trees and flowers understood?
Was it in the hollow of a wave
Before Life came to earth
That our wandering selves met
Waiting for the winds of birth?

Have I been in other times
The blade of grass
Bending in your wake,
The passing cloud
Following your shade,
Or the still pond
Reflecting your image,
Begging life to hasten the years
When at last
I should have the face and the eyes
That could see and feel yours?

Who knows
Or who can tell
Whether in the ages to come
The silence will be broken,
The enigma explained
And the vision fused into harmonies
Which no earth can hold?

Whatever has been
Or whatever will be,
Gapes into darkness,
What remains
Is that along your pale veins
Time slowly moves,
Pervading the sands,
Until appearances are changed
And our images melt into the fire
Whence will surge others.

MIST

I walk and feel in my veins the weight of the sun,
Around my throat a desert wind burns,
My ears echo with the sounds of obsessing drums,
And my eyes reduce the world to a rising flame.

I live in the blaze of noon, unmindful of the rain,
And the mist flows round my face, golden
Like the tropical sands which consume
My hands following the lines of desert dunes.

The earth, like a boundless ocean, rises
Round my heart, timeless point in a tide
Which drives the throbbing flowers and the stars
Through the passion of endless fires.

JOURNEY UNDER THE SEA

Do not sail on Thursday.
The weather was bad,
The black winds were rising,
The sea maddened by the moon
Would not allow an angel's wing
To rest a second on its lashing waves.
Oh do not sail on Thursday!

But Thursday was the date,
Set on the book of days,
The riggings were ready and taut,
The crew were full of hope
And eager to feel on their faces
Salty winds and the scent of receding land;
So, against all odds, we sailed on Thursday.

We waved good-bye to the tall trees,
To the carefree hens and the children
Who paced about the cobbled stones,
We brushed past fat boats
Gaping at our impudent mien,
Laughing at our attempt,
And small busy-bodies envying us,

We watched in the distance
The fading spires of churches,
The houses which we knew,
Smoke-etchings in the sky,
And soon we remained alone
On the wild reels of the waves
With the wind and the sea-gulls.

We reached the open sea,
All things in our boat singing,

And nets and baits lying in wait
For the white moon prize
Which lay in the green fields
Beyond the gorgon waves
And the treadmill we had to tread.

We passed flocks of bulls and calves
Playing with bubbles of foam
Like men and children on grass,
While their wives and mothers weave
Patiently by their sides
The thread-bare hours of waiting,
Regardless of waves and broken hulls.

We raced hump-backed monsters
Sailing with the wind in our direction,
Wondering what force,
What bait could draw us
Through biblical wrath and clouds,
With hisses of salt-beaked birds
And groans of the wailing wood.

The sun had been dead for days,
The curtains were down from the sky,
And the moon and the stars were asleep
In worlds beyond our cries,
Only Venus the white goddess
Had braved storms and waves
And stood still at the prow of the boat.

We had courage and we had vision
Guiding our eyes, luring us
Over the graveyards of time and men,
Amongst the rolling drifts of death
And the howlings of animals and birds
Who knew that our beds were booked
On the banks of the under-sea world.

And so when a wave from the Red Sea
Rolled over us like a molten slab,
We knew that we were bound
For the burning grave where Moses lies,
And where Salomé cuts and kisses
Endlessly the locks and the head
That spoke to the world of eternal Truth.

We shot downwards like mercury in a tube,
Rushing past hideous fins till, like a lift,
Midway we stopped and realized
That from then on, across an infinity of years,
Like foetuses waiting for birth,
We would be lulled by still waves
Where neither hope nor hell can live.

There we were, the whole of us,
The boat complete, except the sails,
Unnecessary to this windless place,
The crew with their memories
As full as the eels that watched them
With their dark hopeless eyes,
Black Venus head down at the prow,

And I, transparent as a Medusa
Reflecting glaucous water,
Following on the distant, restless sands
The graphs of my endless searches
Past and future, realizing at last
That, like a rootless plant,
I could only live in the loom of the waves.

And I wonder if I shall ever again
Hear the wind singing in the sails,
The sea-gulls shrieking for food,
And siren-songs — candles on the waves
Illumining the wound and the shape

Which led us to this storm
And to our boat under the seas.

Will that boat ever glide again
Like a dream bird over the waves,
Will it once again race the sea-horses
Towards harbours where church steeples
Pierece the clouds, and where I walked
With songs in my head
And the Summer sun in my hands,

Will I ever see the morning star
Trailing her wound across the sky,
Asking me to leave all and the shore
To follow her once more to her algae bed?
What for, why should I feel again the wood
Shuddering under my feet
And the icy winds cutting the face?

Why break once more the transparency
Of the bones and the heart — prophet
Of all things, past and future —
When they have been for years the toys
Of the earth and of the fire of the blood?
Ah, let them now be, for Time's length,
The toys of the waves and silence,

Let them live and not live,
What can only be lived in briny veins,
Let them lull through stillness
Venus asleep in her transparent flesh,
And let them wait for the hour
When the black sun will at last
Reduce sea and earth to night.

THE UNFAITHFUL

The night was deep and dark,
The stars looked down from the silent sky,
I lay still on a river bed
Watching boats sliding over my head.

I waited for countless years
Dreaming of the sea, emerald green,
Mother of the white goddess
With the flowing flaxen hair.

One day when the ancient river
Stopped its course towards the waves
And the clouds, I saw your face
White beyond the waters, still as glass.

I could not believe my eyes that you had returned,
You could not believe yours that I had lived,
And I took you away among the stars
And laid you down on a bed of flowers.

I lifted your moon-white face in my hands
And drank the slow fire of your lips
As from a magic cup which one breaks
Once the wine has been drained away.

I borrowed for you the horses of the sun,
And riding along the Milky Way,
Beyond Cassiopeia and the Gemini,
I took you to nameless constellations.

Flames and ice wrapped my mind,
And swept across marble plains and ridges
In a strange voyage beyond words,
Lulled by the tides of your sea eyes.

When at last I woke from this timeless flight
From the tropics to the polar frosts,
I saw a dark adder hidden under the grass
And on your face traces of alien rights.

I saw that the sun of ancient years
Had consumed you away to a dried husk
And that nothing remained except the gaze
Of hollow eyes sunk in the stony past.

By the look you gave me, I understood
That Heaven had for long been lost
And that the woman who with me had lived
Among the stars, had only been the loan of a moment.

Strange hopelessness of things done,
Of love born and found, too late,
I was the lover you lost, centuries before,
I shall sleep now, until rivers run no more.

LET THERE BE PEACE

Between us, let there be peace at last,
For lo, the oases lie far away, lost
In the mist of distant days
When rose in our veins the force
Which grows white in the apple-trees
And weaves in the throats of birds
The sun-thread of golden hours.

Let us cease to regret and to grieve
For the flowers lost and the rosy dawns
Of seasons when in all buds or leaves
Shone the innocence of children's eyes;

Let us now join our strength to cross
The desert with the single compass of Death,
And the memories of tomorrow's vales.

New dawns will rise, new stars will shine,
But our roses gnawed by the worms
Will never again pervade the breath of Spring
With strewn petals exhaled in joy;
They are dying, and they know it,
And no self-willed sap can bring them life,
They can only wait for the Winter winds
To weave with their ashes the everlasting song.

MARBLE-DREAM

Only shells echoing the sounds of distant shores
And hollow night torn by the winds of lost spells;
Where is now the murmur of words which rose
With the swell of your ocean eyes,

Where is the breeze which laden with the scent
Of your cedarn hair could make trees
Dance, and roll my singing head
Across the floor of silent seas?

Where are the coral isles, sweeter
Than red must of newly-made wine,
Where are the pale blue veins, mysterious rivers
Flowing inward, pointing the way to lost travellers?

Where are the sails, where is the vessel
Which could follow the revolutions of the stars
And, in the wake of the sun, burn with a flame
Which had never known night?

Now, only night, ever rent by your white
Living marble slipping through my burning
Hands, hoary salmon sliding
Back into the waves of my restless sleep.

SPRING

When the sun sings in trees, and gilds
The face of dormant ponds,
When green spreads with the new breath
Of the earth,
Then leaves grow from my green hands
And grass gropes from my million roots,

Then my infinite selves, memories
Of translunar voyages, rise
On wings pierced by the light
Which broke the thick night
In the grey dust of the olive groves.

Spring is the dying, into the force
Which drives the stars through their course,
And the blood to stones,
It is the hollowness of the years lost,
And the growth of flowers from eyes
Once loved, now latched by lasting lids.

Spring is the sad song
Of faded words and distant winds,
The dirge from the throat of birds
And the life-long dream dissolved
Into the falls of the April rains.

Spring is the time of pains,
The time when the shining sun
Shows the cracks in the wall
And the rising sap, the broken veins
Of trees laden with years,
It is the time when with a long
Backward glance, I look
Beyond the seas where I have lived,
To my islands lost, and wait
For the waves and the last white rose.

ST. PETER'S SWORD

Said the Master to the disciple:
'Do not strike, for I came to cure, not to kill,
The fall is the fall of man, not of Satan;
There is no Satan; no angel, my Father-born,
Could ever be anything else but good,
Since my Father is wholly so;
And if angels came from another world,
It would be a denial of my Father's power.
There is nothing but Heaven in Eternity,
And Hell is man's longing for unity;
Adam was born good and remained so;
And why should he not, fresh from the womb
With God's breath flowing all over his limbs
And his mind filled with heavenly dust,
Why should he not dream of what he had lost?
Poor Satan, poor serpent, poor Eve,
What loads of tales have fallen with the apple leaves!
Yet Adam and Eve did what they were made for;
And the serpent! . . . ah, the serpent: he crawled,
Since he could not fly or swim as before,
But why make of him the sin of Satan who never lived?
The story is simpler, yet more crude,
Without blaming Adam or any fallen son of God.
It all began when men spelled their needs,
When they left the solitude of the briar woods
To gather in caves or in stone-built holes,
More concerned with their skins than with their souls.
While, before, they might have knocked each other down
Trying to climb the same tree or to catch the same
Fawn, in the same way as crows strive
For the possession of the same flesh, dead or alive,
Their skill increased their needs and their greed,
And the elemental blow with which the tiger killed

Became the lethal way of this wild world
Where God's grace lies buried beyond the reach of thought;
And I have come to wash away with my blood
This layer of lies, and, pouring my sorrow without stint,
To bring men back to the purity of Adam,
I have come to wipe out all sins except one —
To kill, I have come to bless all failings,
Even Judas' kiss, I have come to tell
You all that since there is such a distance
Between my Father's white and the dark vale
In which men live, all must be forgiven
Except the knife in another man's breast;
With one wide-spreading move of my eyelids
I could break more Philistine heads
Than Samson and all those who pulled
Upon themselves the walls of their temples,
Yet these heads were human heads, and I will
Not, I will not wave a finger to prove my strength;
I shall overwhelm, transform the wide earth
With the salt of my tears, the redness of my blood
And the long hours I shall endure the spear
In my heart and the vinegar in my mouth;
My Father never kills, He only unfolds life,
And His name can never be used to cover tombs;
Now and for time's length, I shall never bless
Those who kill, even with a cross in their hands.
And if in a cold, loveless world I were to decide
Which one I disliked least between the soldier
Who kills for his beliefs and his pride,
And the calm indifference of the cool gladiator
Who, passionless, gives his life for bread
Or gambles it in a dance of the sword,
My choice and pity would rather go to those
Who, amongst themselves, or against beasts,
Receive or give death as a holocaust
To tomorrows which have nothing to offer.'

GRAVEYARD BY THE SEA
(17th century cemetery, Monreith)
To Robert Speaight

Surrounded by rocks, bristling with trees,
At the sea's edge between water and stones,
A handful of graves overwhelmed by thorns
Have stood centuries of invading seas;

Above, the cliff hangs threatening and sullen
Keeping watch over these lone lingering dead;
Below, the insidious sea seeks to creep unseen
Towards the last remains of a ghostly land.

Here is no quiet roof for walking doves,
The wandering sea with the moon in her heart,
Restless lover of the rocks and the grey graves,
Heaves and withdraws her waves, all passion spent;

No justice, no sun pours down its golden rays
From the noon-day sky; most things are grey,
The sea laced with a whirlwind of foam,
The sky cold and gaunt like the hangman's dawn,

The rest is green with the growing fields
Whose ageless sleep is disturbed by steely streams,
Bracken, bramble bushes and nettles
That have cornered these lonely stones.

Here the wind of the whirling earth never ceases,
It bends the crooked backs of trees
Flat against the ground in an endless climb,
And sweeps forward their hair, denying their roots.

Some reach the top, others remain behind,
Bare bones of forlorn supplicant hands
Raised above the graves and the ruins of an old chapel,
Lacquered in green like the hulk of a heraldic boat.

Here, amongst riotous winds and days of green and grey
The only white is the spray of the sea,
Floating veil of gauze over the graves
And their sleepy world of mouldering dreams,

Here, insects cannot sing or scratch the dust,
They can only crawl over dank weeds
And slimy stones, or burrow their way back to the past
Amongst empty skulls and husks of lids,

Here too one wonders where are the eyes that looked seaward,
Listening to the sound of lips no longer heard,
Where is the crimson colour of love and the berries,
Where is the black or gold of the loved hair?

All has faded into the greyness of Time,
The scent of flowers and the flames of love,
And nothing remains of tears and laughter
Except the rain in dishevelled groves,

And here, as elsewhere, we meet the worms,
Inane lodgers of wise men's heads,
Or erratic lovers of those famed feminine arms
Which in the shade of the gods shook the frame of the world.

Yet here, where the vision is barred by the rain,
Where earth, sea and sky melt into mist,
The rain falls from the eyes, the sea flows along the veins,
Stones regain the lost lime from the living bones,

Man and nature fade into one thing which dimly feels
That the sea rolls into its waves all the words fallen
From age-long faded lips, that the rocks are not as still
And as immutable as man's living soul,

And that until sea and rocks melt into one,
Until the earth regains its former light
Or rejoins the undying remains of burnt-out fires,
Death sleeps, and will only die with the end of night.

DESTINY

We walk with the sun at our back,
Our destiny precedes us,
Unavoidable, eternity-made
Shadow of a substance which illumines
The human roads, and moulds
The starry shores of Heaven
As the ocean the earthly sands.

The power which whirls the planets
Round their suns and galaxies,
Whirls our blood through our arteries,
Our minds through the maze
Of Labyrinths, as straight as lines
For the White Virgin with the boundless eyes
Who unreels Time from the palm of her hand;

Webs more finely spun
Than the finest silk, we wonder
At the thickness of the thread
Which binds together man
And the primal trees,
The last cloud and the first flower,
We wonder, but in vain, what Minotaur,
What three-headed monster
Shelters behind the seven doors
Locked by the breath of the dying sun.

PROCESSION

(Whit Walks in Manchester)

The procession begins to move, first the beadle
Carrying high above the crowd, the riddle
Of two thousand years, the gaunt face
With the great gashing wound in the breast,
The hole which the blood-sucking lips
Of all the Philistines of this lost planet
Have burrowed in the heart of the dying God.

Then, in the shade of the hollow ribs,
Below the long lean arms raining red,
With their wonder-struck eyes and golden heads,
White-robed and with flowers in their hands,
The little ones, the lost, the blest,
Those who can still spell fables on dead leaves
And hear angel-choirs in the throats of birds,
The innocent, the underfed, those whose faces
Have just been washed for this great day
For them to tread the blue lanes of the skies
Dreaming of gold and silver dresses, of toys,
Of trains, horses and boats rushing past
Like processions in a profusion of stars,
Moving along mountains of cakes and shores
Where sweets like pebbles fill every grove
And roll with the murmur of the waves.
But they can only have the dream
While the world goes by, like shadows
On a screen, in front of their dazed eyes;
The end of the day will bring them back
To the empty scuttle by the black hearth,
To the glare of stark light on bare walls,
To the lonely bun on the naked board
And tea dripping down from dented cups
With drops which in two thousand years

Should have pierced the heart of man.
Was it for this that He came to earth and died,
Was it to be taken out for a yearly walk
Along flower-decked streets filled with songs
Rising from hollow chests where no heart beats?

And the procession continues.

                                        After the cross
The priests, or the ministers; for what does it matter
Whether they wear black robes or surplices?
They all claim to know the mystery of the Birth
And of the loss which cost us our earthly joys,
And they walk with rock-like faces
In the light of the sun, while naked swords
Shine from their thousand hands.

Let the children die of starvation,
Let them roam in grimy streets
In search of bliss which they will only find in sleep,
Or let them go to their holes to ache and cough
Away by their fathers' beds lungs
Ground by dust and the indifference of love,
Let men defile the face of the earth
And murder one another in gold braids
With all the means the human mind
Has been able to devise, while they,
The ministers, the parsons and the priests,
Of all the vast lands which Christ
Reclaimed with the dew of His blood,
In English, Russian or French words,
Indifferently bless the flags and the loads
Of fire which from the air fall on stunned heads,
And the holocaust of men who have just begun
To feel on their faces the first flush of Spring.

And the procession continues.

                    Through the streets,
Throughout the ages, through the bleeding heart
Of man and the ruins where he lives.
After the priests, the parsons, the ministers,
The notables with their chains of office,
The successful, those who have climbed up,
With soft-padded feet, the last rungs of the ladder,
Those who have been able to shut their eyes
To the glare of harrowing sights, and their ears to cries,
Those who have been single-minded,
In the shadow of God, so they say,
Those who cursed sin, yet sinned,
But were never caught; for there is the rub —
Sin we all may, but to be caught!
Only fools, weaklings or madmen can sin
And be caught, sin and proclaim it in the face of the sun!

And the procession continues.

                    After the cross,
The children, the church and the notables,
The well-groomed, well-fed, well-thinking people,
Those dressed in morality from top to toe,
Those who see Christ as a dominie
Or as a policeman with the chastising rod,
And His Father as the judge of the ruthless scales;
Those who think that hearts may justly bleed
And bones may burn as tarred bodies
In inquisitions or city walls in the blaze of war,
As long as the flames and the red are
Neatly buried under the shroud of the Law.

Who said: 'Thy sins are all forgiven thee',
And who said: 'The breath divine is love'?
'Christ? — Perhaps; but then He forgave
So many things and people — Magdalene and Mary,
He forbade violence, He kissed Judas' lips,

He lived amongst rogues and prostitutes,
He forgot the Sabbath, He forsook His parents
And, wanderer without a home, He lived
With love in His heart and God above
Watching His lamblike sacrifice to redeem
The lost children of Adam.
But Christ is only a name, a shape,
Cross-wise, outstretched arms, not to kiss,
But to point the way or to chastise
Those who lapse into love of neighbours,
Or enemies who have not been approved by the Law.
O Moses, Christ could remove the stone
Which stood at the entrance of His tomb and return
To His heavenly Father, but He could not lift
The whole twelve heavy, monumental slabs
Of your burning Laws which now crush the world!
And the convict-Christ, bearing their marks
On His shoulders, with halting steps and broken heart,
Walks away in solitude, is carried away
In solitude.

Who then follows Him?

The procession continues.

                        Last come the poor,
The forlorn, those whom hope has deserted at the gate
Of their birth, the travellers of the desolate moors
Of the earth, those who are always too late
For the manna or the light of the stars,
Those who do not feed on the food of life
But on the opium of dreams to forget the strife
And the sorrows which they drag at their feet,
Those who ache and die with words of love
On their lips, those who in distant lands
Or in hovels bleed for causes they do not understand,
Those who have never sat on Moses' chair

And followed with a faltering finger
The Minoan intricacies of the Law,
The innocent, the pure, those whom the Minotaur
Tears to pieces as the yearly tribute paid
For the sophistry of Athens, the defeated,
The condemned under the Law, the roofless
Under the slabs which crush their hearts
And let in hail, wind and rain,
All those who, above the hooded guides and the well-fed,
Above the notables and Moses' head,
Beyond the haze of twenty centuries, can see Christ
In the distance, and slowly walk in His wake
Towards the Eden-town where the apple tree
With its blossom of love and truth
Will bring them joy and the fruit of their faith
Through the long naked night, and the reward for woes
Endured under the granite of laws,
And for the offering of their hearts
As the only food which could feed others
And bring them back to the divine Law-Breaker.

And the procession continues.

IF I WERE NOT SURE

If I were not sure that you have been,
And will be again, in worlds where my hands
And heart will hold at last the shape
Which my eyes in this life have seen,
Sorrows would rise like the tidal seas
And drain away my self to the depths of despair,
To dark waters where the sun never rises,
To oceans without waves or shores.
But I know that what has been once, for ever is,
And that if I could turn the centuries like the pages
Of a book, I would find, somewhere amongst the leaves
Of yesterday or tomorrow, your image
      And mine, as old as light, and casting upon the earth
        That single shadow of which forever we have dreamt.

TRYING TO WRITE

When I grope in vain along the sparry hollows of the mind
In search of thoughts and visions which may live in plays,
My heart, following the Ariadne-thread of your hand,
Leads me to dream lands, the longings of my eyes;
At each bend of the road shines the light of your face,
Golden moss and the chasms of this underworld landscape
Become your hair and the curves of your haunting shape,
Your eyes like stars pierce the dark of the long lanes,
Rippling waterfalls sing with the music of your voice,
And over lost green nooks or bowers of silence
Where nothing lives, floats the fragrance of your name.
Then caught in a web which no force can break,
Wayworn, cloud-borne, weary of struggling
Against the eagle-wings of your high soaring love,
I close my eyes and drop towards unknown worlds
To come to rest on the waves of your lulling breast.

FLIGHT OF A BIRD

Tonight the flight of a bird disturbs my sleep,
I lie awake counting the stars, white pearls
Across the skies where, lost, a woman weeps,
Tears roll slowly down the Milky Way and fall
On the face of the earth furrowed by tides of sorrow;
The silent world sleeps except for the rustle of leaves,
Trembling birds longing for the sun of tomorrow,
And a throbbing heart which in the dark grieves.
    Yet I know for certain that dawn will rise
    Over troubled seas and calm mountains,
    And that the moment when I meet your eyes
    Will drown in their waves all worries and pains,
        For I have never known in my heart a wound
        Which could not be healed by the touch of your hand.

DARK OF NIGHT

When in the dark of night I walk
With all my senses in my heart blind,
When birds and chiming clocks
Mock the muffled sounds of my beating mind
Telling me that beyond the grief of groping hours
And the piercing pain of eyeless sight,
Whether on earth or amongst the stars,
The day will ever follow the obsessive night;
Then your words from nowhere rising
Bring me the force to wait for your absent face,
And the thought of your love so pure and moving
The strength to be worthy of your praise,
    So that in the end I feel that with you I am one
    And that I live and can only live by you alone.

LOVERS' TALK

One night on a moonlight walk
I heard two lovers talk:
'Oh why worry', said she,
'Why not vary the curve of the lips,
Why not be sad or merry
According to whether we bite
The pulp or the bitter pips
Of the apple of our endless love?
Why not be like leaves
Blown by the wind, why fear
Since days more numerous
Than the sheaves of Croesus' harvest
Fill the rafters of the roofs
Where shelter our newly-born lives,
Why refuse tears or rain
If tóday they come,
When we know that tomorrow
Will bring again the warm sun?'

'Because, my dear, my dear,
Just as green grass dies
And the sun fades in clouds of fear,
Shadows may fill your eyes
Before you can even shed a tear
For sorrows that have been wrought
When unhappiness like a sour fruit
Made you distort into a grin
The smiling face of Heaven;
Because the faint throbs of your pulse
May at any moment stop in your sleep
Before you can, with a last word,
Wipe away from memory's board
The bitter traces of unwanted grief,
And because any morning you may discover,
Stunned with horror and fear,

That the spots that stain your skin
Mark your impending end under the sun;
So my dear, my very dear,
Whether we are eyes to eyes,
Or stretching hands over the seas
With the white faith of lovers
Over whom Death has no power,
Let us always meet and say good-bye
As if the next moment we were to die.'

TELL ME

Tell me, if you know, what things
In the heart grow, that can bring
Us both on the same side of the truth;
Tell me what song I must sing,
What mandrake root you must drink
To awaken into a world of delight
Where love and wonder are the only lights.

Tell me what lanes of the sky I could explore,
What stars and comets I could gather
To lay them on your lap like jewels
Which will, for endless moments, reflect
The gold of your eyes and the diamond-days
Slipping through your sieve-like fingers
Like freckled fish in mountain rivers.

Tell me what golden fleece of words I should weave
To bring to your heart the tides of heavenly seas
And into your hands the treasures of eternal sands,
To make you tremble with joy and believe
In the truth, that only the golden apple of the Hesperides
Can ripen and live throughout the infinite summer
Of the evergreen hills of the elysian world.

INTO YOUR HANDS

Into your hands lay my head
And all the drops of my restless blood
Which from tropic to pole follow your moods,
Feathers in the wind or heavier than lead.

Under your smile melts the pain,
As melts the ice under the sun,
As fades away in the evening breeze
The melancholy dance of autumn leaves.

At your angel-voice the burning winds
Of the solar seas and the dark wings
Of dewy stars crowing to the morning light
Are hushed back into the mouth of night.

PARTING

Every night they stand by the same wall
Trying to hold up with a last kiss the dark
And the scalpel-hour dividing the heart
In two parts drowned deep into Lethe dull.

In their eyes the terror of the long evening and the hours
To be ground away till the sun rises
In the late afternoon, and pours its golden rays
On a world where pavements teem with flowers,

In their hearts, swelling seas rising
To break on the shores of night strewn
With the hulk of hollow dreams and longings
White as the haunting face of the waning moon,

And by their side, as if to offer them the balm
Of its perfume and the hope of other climes,
An apple tree with its wisdom of white blossom
Bends its venerable head over their tidal woes.

WITHOUT YOU

Without you, I breathe, I grieve,
I eat, and seek in sleep
The rest and the oblivion deep
Which nothing but you can give.
Within myself no force can lift
The weight of sorrow and night
Which doubly weighs upon my mind
And fills my heart with sighs
For the light of your blest eyes.

Without you the arrow-hours
Ever pierce my Sebastian-heart
Amidst songs of birds and flowers
Bleeding with life, longing for death
And for the bliss of the lost breath,
For I can only live and rise
In the light of your blest eyes.

Life without you is not life
But the void filling the hours
Until I return to you, beloved,
To lull love's sweet wound
On the white waves of your breast,
And to dissolve my cares
In the light of your blest eyes.

MY HEART

When through days I walk,
My mind walled by your thoughts,
Each step stumbling against your face,
Each thing smiling with your smile,
Hours lengthen into eternal years
And the moment I shall see you recedes
Into the hoary end of the frozen earth.

Then my heart trembles in terror
At the thought of the distance which lies
Between this moment of death and rebirth,
And seeks in vain refuge in your image.

But my heart has no voice, no means
To live the rise and fall of lovers' talks,
For the blood which flows in my veins
Whispers with your words, and my hands
Only know the force of your living shape,

So that harrowed by ever-renewed pain,
Dweller of a house where nothing of me lives,
I watch, from the last recess of my mind,
The strange moves of a heart which is no longer mine.

YOUR GIFTS

You came to me like the goddess of spring,
Your arms full of flowers, your eyes full of stars,
Purer than lilies or the first morning
When the great wings moved slowly over the waters,

You rose white as foam from the innocent waves,
Dewy pearls dropping from your golden head,
The sinuous curve of your lips, trembling leaves
In the infinite roar of celestial winds.

You came to me with more gifts in your wake
Than waves in the trail of the silent moon,
And without a word, for Love's sake,
You gave them all, more angel than woman.

How shall I ever sing, beloved, the glow
Of your face and the force which rises
From the gold of eyes deeper than the seas,
Source of a life which Death can never kill,

How could I ever forget gestures like violets,
A faith as great as any heart can hold,
And the sweetness of a light which shapes nights
And days into the drowsy bliss of an endless dream?

LAZARUS' LAMENT

I wish I could sing with the tongue of the dead,
I wish I could tell of old men's grief,
Of wisdom wasted in men's desert hearts,
Of words blown in the wind like random leaves,
I wish I could unseal young men's lips
And release from the icy lands where they burn
The words unsaid and the bridal sighs
Which sing in the lights of the polar sun,
I wish I could smooth away from the Earth's face
The wrinkles and ruins of daemonic nights,
The smouldering fires of Judean hills
And the cancerous growth which since Hiroshima
Eats up her throat.

From my grave, with the earth on my head,
I can see dust rising over deserts
Where God lies dead, and the stellar cold
Gripping a world maddened with power and gold,
I can hear the cries of men rolling their heads
Along muddy lanes, or heaping stones
Upon their hearts to stifle their moans
Sadder than any wind in winter nights;
I wish I were in the limbo world
Waiting for dawn and Christ the God,
Sweeter than milk on the morning table.

Oh! Where are the gods and goddesses of Greece,
Hermes of the magic wand and winged feet,
Venus with the foam and sapphire face,
Athene with the olive branch, and the thought
Which brought Orestes to the groves of peace?
Where is Zeus with the lightning eye,
Where is Artemis for whom Endymion died,
Apollo with the flaming hair, and the hand

Which led the fiery race across the sky,
Where is she who moved with doom in her name
And, in spite of Time's rending wound
And the grey dust which dims her eyes,
Remains the world's ever reborn dream,
Where is the fire which burrowed her bones
And the kiss that burnt Trojan walls
And lifts the earth on the wings of Spring?
Where is Ulysses, more than man, dear to Zeus,
Wilier than the gods, and with a heart
Which could listen to the siren's song and leave,
To climb steadily the long stairs of waves
Which barred the way to his journey home?
Above all, where is Herakles, son of lust
And Alcmene with the soft heart,
Where is he, the God-man who, without fall,
Twelve times lifted His cross and walked
To Judas of the long hair and the shirt of flames,
Which since Adam has consumed man's soul
And will burn beyond the waters of the grave?
Where are they all? Dead under the waves,
Or buried under the hills and the trees,
In the hollow of skulls which gave them life,
Or asleep perhaps, in hammocks of gauze
Tied to the moon and the stars, beyond the strife
Of the earth's tempests and tidal waves!

Sons of Kronos, sons of man
Struggling to unite the atoms of chaos,
They could not survive the claws of Time,
They had to die with the eyes
Which descried them in sacred groves,
Or on the banks of rivers, and made them live
On the Eleusinian shores and in the Acropolis.
Neither Plato's wisdom nor the bitter end of Socrates
Could pour light into the hollow stare

Of statues with which men had tamed nature;
Christ the God-man had been with them
Since the beginning, under the fur of the ape,
In their long nights, their journeys across the steppes
Of Time, their straightening up of the bent spine,
And their faces turning white like the marble
Of the Aegean hills; they could always feel Him,
And they had moved away from fear to faith,
Coming nearer and nearer to the white of Truth,
Yet the great force which could fuse into oneness
Zeus' lightning and Apollo's flaming horses
Had not been revealed to them; for how could they
With their human eyes span the infinite sky?

So God the Father, above the Olympian heights,
Realizing man's solitude and his plight,
Decided to stretch His guiding hand
To the dearest of His creatures, the only one
Who could ache and rejoice with a mind
Which Death could never own;
And gathering His will from the vast universe
Which He controls, He concentrated it
Like a shaft of light on a spot of the earth,
At a moment of mankind's life, in the shape
Of a man, so that all men could see Him
And remember throughout Time
His words, His image living in everyone,
That they might see at last what was
And would always be, in their eyes, in their hearts.

I have seen all, I have been with Christ
Since the beginning, I have been
The knowing, silent part of man,
The memory of God which could never remember
God except in Christ, for how could I
Remember what had no past,

How could I see what was pure vision
And I part of light? I have seen reflections
Of flames fade away into darkness
And God's light lost in the white of space,
Until some rays struck the stained mirror
Of man's soul and sent back to their Source
The first glimmers of the unknown timeless face;
I have seen how men's eyes sealed
By the Lethean glare of darkness
Could only stand the glow of Christ's light,
I have understood how the living and the dead,
The air and the lungs where it will burn,
The void left in space for the flower's shape,
The phantasmal shades of thoughts and deeds
Waiting to rise in the wake of the absent breath,
And all things blind in the vast womb
Where night and day burn without shadows,
Where protons and neutrons of unborn cells
Wheel endlessly like Saturn's rings
Round a centre filled with unnamed forms,
Are like drifting wood or boats caught in eddies,
Watching through cyclonic silence
Life's current blindly sweeping past,
And will never feel the embrace of the living sea;
They breathe an absent air, and they will never live,
For nothing ever is, which has not been
Through Christ and the aches of Time.

And Christ came and a glorious light wrapped the earth
And illumined the grave where, for long, I had lain
And lived among the dead; I rose and walked
In the wake of the magic voice, towards a birth
More cruel than any death; for after the joyful dawn
And rainbow-coloured hopes, came the grey light of the moon,
The disembodied world in which I had to live,
The unbearable truth of men walking with death in their bones,

Spreading round them a smell of long decayed coffins
That was stronger than all the fragrance of spring;
So in this world of dead on leave,
I longed for the perfume of the grave, and I said:
'Oh Christ who know that there will be no second coming,
And that all the blood which is to flow from your aching veins
Cannot wash away for Time's length the scars of men's stains,
Oh Christ, why did you bring me back from the dead
Since my rebirth will be my death?
Why did you cut with your words the roots
With which I clasped the anaesthetized earth,
Why did you recall to my frozen limbs
The diffused force which makes the earthly spring;
Why have you re-awakened in my slumbering mind
The harrowing pangs of the kingdom of the dead?
Was it pity that answered my sisters' prayers,
Was it love that moved you, the dearest of brothers?'
And closing my eyes, I can see the beloved face
And hear the soft, yet already far away voice:
'I do not know why; I cannot say
Whether it was love, pity, both, or neither;
Perhaps it was a last desperate impulse
In the face of a slowly closing world
Of truth untold, perhaps I felt that at this and only time
Death had to be defeated, and that I had to tear
From the thickening weight of lime
A being, a forlorn brother, the image of my fate.

Perhaps I wanted to test my strength
In a last throw, although I know that in the end
I cannot win, for such is my Father's will,
And I can only ask for the force to endure it all;
I know and do not know, yet I fear,
For I hear the vast womb of the earth claiming me,
I hear the growing roars of crumbling worlds,
I know that the great moment is at hand,

The last and most difficult of moments,
And lost, afraid perhaps, I brought you back
From your strange, lightless silence,
You the dearest of my brothers,
As a gesture of defiance to death
Which will overcome me, and perhaps to hear
From the only one who knows, what courage
It requires to face the last lonely hour.'
And I who had lived it all and knew
That the dreaded night was drawing near,
I, who could hear the jingling coins
In the silence of trembling stars,
See the beads of sweat in the torches' glare
And hear the name which sends sham shudders
Down the spine of the ages, I, with sad tears, said:
'Oh Master, divine Master, God's grace
To guide us back to the eternal light,
Master, you need all your courage,
For the moment when the blood turns to stone
In the veins, the moment when the mind gasps
For the fading light, is a terrifying one,
And I, whose love for you is as old as the birth
Of the earth and the stars and will outlive them,
Would do anything to spare you this bitter hour;
For, if I am the only one who will have to die twice,
You die endlessly with every stain of men's life,
Yet the death which you will soon know,
The tearing apart of life, the breaking up of cells
Brought together in the light of the sun,
Their dispersion to the four winds of Heaven
Until Judgment Day, is the cruellest of all,
The one which might bring us our Father's grace;
For how can He who never dies
And will never know the lovelessness of the grave
Know what death is and what pity it deserves?
Only His son, yet truly man, doubting His might,

Wrenched by suffering, wondering why, can enable Him
To know what it is, and to forgive all the failings
Of man's life which the agony of death redeems.
And I who know what it is, pity you,
For, although God on earth, you will suffer
The death of man, the death which no god can soften
At the final point when body and mind agonize alone;
We all know that death will not last, but yours
Will be the hardest, for it will be all deaths in one,
And through you, from your infinite eyes,
Will fall all the tears of human sorrow, the tears
Which will for ever redeem piteous man.'

And I remember how in His eyes deeper than the seas
Floated the great shadows of things to come,
And how the sad sigh which heaved His sorrowful breast
Echoed in my knowing heart with the cry of the night
In the olive grove when His cells were shaken by fear;
I remember his words to Judas of the mediating kiss,
The words which I had known since my birth:
'Oh Judas, forlorn brother, I pity you for my death
Which self-righteous men, longing to blame
And to condemn other men to eternal flames,
Will ever ascribe to your evil mind and money lust
And to the wiles of what they call Satan,
Yet your deed was born with the dawn of Time
And I have for ever known all and the torture
Which for the love of men I had to endure.
Your name was coined together with mine
When my Father's divine breath
Parted waves from clouds, the earth from the moon,
And broke silence with sound and infinity with birth.
Everything had to be from my Father's heart —
Pure diamond, knot of light containing all,
The unborn and the unknown, the ideal and the real,
Until Time and birth stained the still-centred wheel.

But, there is no rebel that Omnipotence
Could not crush; whatever lives —
Light and shadows, tears and joys —
Lives and dies in the light of the eternal eye.
I have come to show you all that evil
Must be accepted, suffering endured,
In order to rise and to return whence we all came,
I have come to show men that there is no room
For condemnation, only room for compassion,
For pity, whatever the road we have to tread,
Whether it is that of Magdalen, Barabbas the robber,
Or yours which led you to the necessary soldiers
Who already knew, and to the waiting cross.
I pity you, whose name will be pilloried by the ages
For having been told at the dawn of the earth,
When your dispersed cells were roaming the vast:
'You will be Judas, the betrayer of Christ.'
Oh poor Judas, how I suffer for you, I who know
That the silver of evil fame is only the symbol
Of a flaw which is inherent in man, I who know
That you yourself are nothing more than a name,
A husk which must henceforth represent for men
The evil impulses which assail many of them.
So why curse you, why condemn you? Come,
Let me wipe away with one kiss the blame
Which men will henceforth set on your sad face,
Let me show you by my tears, dear Judas,
That whatever men or rebel angels may do
To me or to others, I will always understand and bless.'

Oh beloved Christ, what wisdom, what courage
In the acceptance of all the gestures He had to make
And to endure, to show men how to forgive
All the violence which some of them wreak
On others, and the sorrows they have to outlive
So that the good and the bad, light and darkness

May be accepted as part of the everlasting wisdom;
I remember His bitter agony, for it was also that of God,
I remember His descent into the underworld,
His three long nights among the dead
And the new dawn when, with His outstretched arms
In the flaming light of all the joyous stars,
He rose to the burning bosom where He now lives
And feels, for time's length, all the sorrows of men;
I remember the waiting for my second death,
Longed for, in a world of increasing desolation,
Endured to a greater depth than before,
For I knew and could feel in advance the fire
Where the cut of the dark knife was going to fall,
And I remember how on the great wings of my two deaths
I tried to soar to the white point where there are no pains,
But in vain, for I still feel the weight of lime
And, with tortured Christ, I still suffer among men.

What harvest have men gathered, what sheaves
Of golden wheat have they stored from love infinite?
None, except thorns and bitter tears
Which like Tantalus' waves can never
Moisten their parched lips;
Like eyeless worms in the blaze of noon
They no longer see the light, and their hands
Pierced with the wounds of the hanged God
Stain with red the gold they touch
And the high towers of the Juggernaut
Which with indifference they climb to crush
The image of Christ that moves the wheels.
Hollow as the skeleton chiming the hours
That never return, over the earth, they walk
Wrapped in their dreams of drugged oblivion,
Blind to beggars in rags who, with sad looks,
Scan windy lanes for crumbs of food,
Like hungry birds in the winter cold.

Oh, mortal hearts which can only truly live
In the womb of the earth whence spring
Draws the force that shakes the leaves,
The fruit that makes men and birds sing,
And turns the long night of ice and silence
Into the wild music to which nature dances!
Oh, stony world where the human blood
Has ever to be kneaded into clods
Before God's mercy and Christ's heart
Can live in the angel-faces of flowers!
Oh Death, the healer who changes man's frost
To man into the indifference of the grass
And the cyclic music of spring blossoms,
Lasting Death, welcome me back to the trust
Of the earth, where in your arms I shall sleep,
Waiting for the end of Time — your twin —
And the spring which will awaken together.
In lasting bliss, all men, beasts and flowers!

PELICAN AND TOREADOR

'Hunt the white whale across the widening circles
Of the waves, follow her to the edge of doom,
Live by love, and fear not the phosphorous devils
Who weaved souls on Mephistophelian looms;
There are no devils, and there is no God,
They have long been dead and buried,'
Said fierce Gordon with the club-foot
Or steely Ariel with the soft face;
And Poe and Musset, each in his own language,
Added: 'Never write except with the blood of your heart,
Let your burning pen scorch the white of the page,
Let men's sighs rent the stillness of rocks,
Let clouds crumple like silk in their hands,
And the winds and the waves be sieved or locked
According to the whims of their lordly command;
Bar the sun from the earth, or break Descartes' muzzle
Which fetters imagination, and let it roam wild
Across the universe; grope by your inner light
Where no sun shines, grasp with your expanding heart
All that moves over the surface of the earth,
Above in the empty spaces, or below in its bowels;
Sing, sob, sigh, be the voice or the tears
Which break silence and bring forth the flower
That can only rise and live through the human cell,
Show men that in the heart lies the mystery,
And not in the light of the mind, show them Voltaire's folly,
Show them that willows only weep when men cry,
And stars only cram the sky to express their joy.'

And men listened and they burned and they cried,
Till Gordon died of fever, and Ariel drowned,
Till their children rebelled and said: 'Father,
Why don't you realize that rocks do not care
Whether your heart rejoices, aches or bursts,

Or whether your proud flesh returns to dust?
Trees are trees — the moving speech of the earth,
And man has his words; but the waves and the seas,
In spite of their bitter salt, are not human tears,
They are only the vast mirror in which the sun plays,
Or the compass which slowly rises and falls
With the vagaries of the wandering moon;
So, take your unpretentious place among the ants
And the slow-crawling snails, or, if you like, hop
From tree to tree with the birds, but do not believe
That your wings which can swallow space
Make you more important than falling leaves
Or any other sample of animal species.'

Some said: 'Are the rocks — the cup — more important
Than the waves which move from shore to shore,
From the distant days of Homer, and long before,
To our days of bereavement and discontent?
Is a smile only a grinning of the teeth,
And do the eyes only reflect the visions of the earth
And the sky?' 'Form is all', said Flaubert;
'But form for what? — for feelings wrapt in words,
Or for the idea which sings in the ninth sphere
And which no human mind will ever know?'
And others replied: 'There is no time or space,
Only the mind in its ascending and descending flow,
Only the movement from absence to silence,
Or, there is no mind, only the bubbles and froth
Of subterranean waves as old as Adam on earth.'

'God has died', some say, 'and pity has burst';
And after the land has been laid waste and the skies
Emptied by the explosion of atomized unreason,
After the choking dust and the salt-eaten eyes,
After Hiroshima, Auschwitz, Dachau and Belsen,
And Death which fills the solitude of eastern hills,
Can we still talk of tears? . . . do we still dare

To say that love alone overflows our souls,
Our minds and all? Can we talk of burning feelings
When whole towns have blazed, or of our sufferings
When millions have endured the horrors
Of fire from the air, and of the gas chambers?
How could we talk of sorrows to men with seared hearts?
What could be the weight of a poet's tear
Upon the bitter seas which gall the world?
What is the loss of Charlotte or Lenore
To people who have lost all, and live walled
In the grave waiting blank for the timeless cold?
No poet's cries can break through the clamour
And the maddened howls which now fill the air,
They have no meaning, except as echoes
Of a mysterious world which for ever lives
And dies on the uncharted shores of the soul,
As memories of something deeper than the seven seas.
Sincerity for sincerity's sake is only a dance
Which may amuse but does not move;
The only dance which truly moves is the one
In which rhythm and precision
Are measured by the lightning thrust
Of the bull's deadly horns,
It is the dance in which each step is a risk
Of death, a dice's throw in a cloud of dust;
This is not nimbleness for music's sake,
But art for life's sake, a ritual which reveals
The mystery, a lesson that beauty and truth only live
In the arms of death, at the point when the toreador kills
His opponent and friend, and, with compassionate love,
Exposes his heart and body to the fatal thrust,
Knowing that if he misses his half-pirouette or his bow,
Death will not miss him, and that it is at the moment
When her black wings hover above his fearless brow
And when he trusts his whole life to his craft
And his faith, that Eternity consumes Time,
And that, through the holocaust of art, Beauty is born.

THE EAGLE OF PROMETHEUS

Prometheus Speaks to the Earth

Mother mine, do not cry, by this stained rock
Where naked I lie, chained, with black wings
Battering my face, shrouding the sun,
Rising to the sky with bits of my flesh,
Shuttling back and forth with sharp cries
To my heart, bare, torn by beak and claws,
Ever eaten up, ever sprouting to feed the eagle,
Eager-hurrying to cells sweeter than honeysuckle;
Mother mine, in your blind heart, understand
That this blood which flows all round, or rains
Over my gory wounds from this feathered cloud,
Is the dew which cools and allays my pains,
That the beak which lovingly searches my heart
Reveals its existence, that the pain tears veils
Apart and illumines new plains and heights,
That on the eagle's wings I rise to the sun,
And through its staring eyes, I see visions never known.

In your womb I knew nothing but the bliss of silence,
In the skies, before I stole from the gods the fire
Which your sons require to cross
The predestined steppes of Time, I did not live,
I merely was the rose seed in a mould of leaves;
Under the blood red beak blows, the rose
Has burst forth and its fragrance pierces the universe,
My red petals fall over my limbs or float in the winds,
Each one a leaf from the tree which hides the mysteries,
A ladder, skyward stretched for the ascent to the gods.

The sorrows which sear my soul hymn the road
Which must be marked with the trails of my blood,
And in the ages to come a purer blood will streak
With red the skies and show once more the tortures

Which some of your sons, born for claws and beak
Or the thorny crown, will have to endure;
Yet, remember that their tears and sorrows
Are the blood and pains of the cut prenatal cord,
And that chaos entered them in the great book of birth
As the only way to mark the road which men have to follow.

STRANGE WOMAN

Ah, strange woman, siren of silence,
You want me to bring you virgin lands to rule,
Emerald seas, ships with silken sails
And vision to descry Heaven at one glance.

You want me to scale walls, to fall
On my knees and pray at your feet
To have angel's beauty, eagle's strength,
And Franciscan love to hold you in its folds!

Alas! I am neither knight nor saint,
Neither magician nor paladin,
I am only Prospero without a wand,
And the waves have long drowned the island.

I can only offer you what I own —
Vast expanses of desert sands,
A furrowed heart, and the dreams
Of a sun-obsessed, heedless man.

WHEN YOU WALK

When you walk with desire
Hanging from every window of the sky
Burning you,
When you move like wind on wheat
Bending or raising golden heads
In your wake,
When your footsteps engender heat
Of ancestral corn and fire dances
In the noon sun,
Or when your gold-flecked eyes spill
Around them dreams of falling leaves
In fading light,

Can you hear underground whispers
Of water, or see, deep in the earth,
The seismic waves of worms and moles
Trailing you to the appointed place
Where your beauty will fall to their care?

Can you feel in the air drunk
With the glow of your skin, the conspiracy
Of blood and heart throbbing you forth
To the dark where Penelope waits
To unweave the mystery of your cells?

There your lavish limbs will lie
Indifferent to flowers and cries,
And all the tumult of your ardent ways
Will only feed the liquid fire.

LANGUAGE

Language separates us,
Words are coins for commerce,
Disguising cloaks and epitaphs
Whose secrets enfold our deaths,
So until we meet again by Charon's barque
Or cross bones in neutral loam
And spill our mysteries into the dark
Where truth is woven on still looms,
Fare you well my silent ship,
May your prow swiftly ride the waves
And your keel, caulked with sorrows,
Skim the foam and take you past
The exotic isles and the porphyrized coves
Where bodies burn on golden sands.

FORSAKE

Forsake your make-believe and pretences,
And realise what my world is
By your absence;
Life is perjury and all things prophesy
In vain the face, the lips and eyes
Which I miss;
I move in your self-begotten chaos
And silence which can only be dispelled
By your voice;
You remain ever distant and near
Like a longed-for, remembered perfume,
Pervading the air which I breathe,
You and not you, a rainbow of desires
Caught through the prism of a polarised mind,
Imprint upon my heart — your epitaph.

YOU MOVE AWAY

You move away like a lengthening cross,
Night suddenly falls upon the wound
Of your mouth, setting sun in stilled space
Staining with red the receding world.

Frost descends, a monument splits,
Swallows fly away with falling leaves,
And over the horizon where a world fades
Surges the roar of the seven seas.

NIGHT

Yet I know that in other realms
Where absence and the lost sun
Hollow the hours in burning dreams,
Tears are shed which nothing can redeem;
They flow with the aches of a heart
Which frets and grieves at the gnawing thought
That night is slow in a lonely bed
And at visions which burn under the eyelids.

I can feel these tears falling,
The only words of a heart unarmed,
While mine, haunted by this sorrow,
Caught like a boat in polar floes,
Crawls slowly through hours long as years
And dreams of far-away dawns
And ice-sharp lilies on white mountains.

THE ORDER OF THINGS

Oh, the rage at the indifferent order of things,
That you, who should have come first,
Should have come last! The paradox
Of the tortoise overtaking Achilles, of the heart
Catching up with the arrow of its death,
And of the distance between shadow and substance!

The unforgettable sight of a face
Lit by the glow of a fire, in a world
Dissolved in the wild music of a name
And the nearing roar of emerald deep,
With flames and crumbling walls
Shimmering behind a woman's smile!

And ever since, a grief of longing,
Floating, falling leaf before the eyes,
And the heart — wrung bunch of grapes —
Left to bleed and wither on the stem
Through long summers, till nothing remains
But wrinkled skin and distilled sun!

And over all this, piteous Time heaps winter
Upon summer and snow upon fire,
Watching with sorrow how, lost in studies
Of the mechanism of compulsions and desires,
We circle and twist over the shrinking island
Where, in the end, we shall have to land.

WHY SHOULD YOU?

Why should you believe that I've forgotten
How to play the pipe or sing a tune
Ringing with the melody of your name?
My silence is no more strange
Than the absence of light when the sun
Has sunk beyond a mountain range.

Though it's dark, I know light is,
Shining somewhere on some other part
Of the earth, or asleep in the heart
Waiting for the moment to rise
Out of the dark, life-giving sea
Where you and I will always be.

I move in a maze of appearances,
Blundering insect in a thick grove,
Equation of light, conjunction of love,
Only made visible by your presence
Which keeps me real and tied to earth,
Ever echoing the music of your thought.
I see roses grieving on waves,
Dreams swept by whirlwinds,
And petals adrift in uncharted groves
Or pinned to the depth of frozen ponds;

All things fade away beyond reach
And the shipwreck of aching thought,
Trailing images defying speech,
Glimmers on the edge of the infinite.

MEMORY

Baudelaire was such a one
Who would have plumbed the depth of grief
To recover the first fatal drop
Which caused the ocean where he drowned.

But the stains that sour the heart
Are of indelible ink, and the more
One tries to cleanse them out, the more
They spread to cover all parts.

The human heart cannot unlearn
The sorrows and joys of past days,
Memory cannot be emptied out or torn
Like overfull drawers or calendars.

One can only drown its moans
In the roar of life or the sleep of time,
Yet, a moment's silence or a false move
Always uncovers the lurking grief.

LION AND UNICORN

The first time the lion met the unicorn
In a wood, he fell in love with her;
The unicorn, we know, is a fabled animal,
The dream made flesh, the unreal
Brought down to earth on all fours,
Something rare, difficult to find,
Although it exists; a lion told
Me so.

This was love at first sight,
As truly befits lions and unicorns;
The hazel-eyed animal with grace
In her limbs, constancy in her upright horn,
Was caught in the elusive maze
Of sinewy strength with which the royal animal
Grips the ground and lords over all
The surrounding space.

But love was only a meeting point,
A glade, or a circle of hushed fears
That caged the lion's bounds and roars
Ever dreading the unicorn's distant flights;
For he was of the earth, while light and air
Were her elements, and he could never be sure,
When she rushed in and out of the leaves,
How long he would have to grieve.

He could not follow her in her flights,
And his distress and inability to soar
Came out in strange bouts of anger
When he would wound her, then regret
And explain in his animal language
His sorrows and the source of his rage
At the thought that their worlds revolved
Round different centres,
That he could never own her for him alone,
That he felt at times wedded to the wind,
And that's why the sorrow of being earth-bound,
And the dumb anger which heaved up from below
Into destructive rage against what he could not reach,
Made him, whenever he could, claw
Her unfurred skin, then sob and cry
Over the spilt blood.

LOVE

What has love to do with bitter hours
And sad dreams between earth and moon
Where you and I hurtle through airless worlds
Under the fading disc of a receding sun?

We are caught in a neutral field
Of conflicting gravitational forces,
And, stillborn, we roll through the skies
Tied to the earth by the law of lies.
Inquisitive telescopes plot our course
While we watch from space the fading grass
And the dust of a dead lunar world
Where soon we shall plunge in an endless fall.

THE CRUEL TOWN

This cruel town is a crown of thorns
Which I must wear through endless hours;
Each stone cries, cries my heart a name,
And the longed-for light fills the air.

In slow, chained steps, I move, over a hill,
With beads of thoughts streaming down
My aching mind, each thing a cross which bears
Your image with long nails deep in the soul.

Oh, the painful weary crawl, along a road
Where the feet founder in the glue of memories,
Where each cell splits and strains to break
The endlessly stretching ties of past days.

Oh the bitter grin of the sun which mocks
Silence. the cold blade of the moon
Which stabs to stillness agonies of flames
And the icy winds which dispel paradoxes!

Birds, their beaks wide open, sing no song,
And leaves remain stilled in mid-air;
Time has died, taking away the breath
Which gave joy to birds and compelled leaves to earth.

Alone, Eternity remains, enclosed in a name,
A broken record revolving round and round,
Saying the same thing, which is nothing, at a speed
Such that arrival and departure are always the same.

I wait, and wonder when the world will move again,
When time will rise like the dawn
Out of its stillness, when night will fade
And all things will lose their sameness,

When trees will sing with their million leaves,
When each fruit will recover its primal taste,
Each bird's feather its true colour, and when reborn life
Will burst like a frenzy of stars in the breast.

WHEN I AM GONE

When I am gone from this world
And you are left with my absence
Which will fill so much of you
That you'll be a deceptive husk
Under an unchanging sky,
You'll wonder which of us is alive
And which is dead, for I
Shed all but appearances

From the moment I met you
And became a dissembling image
For all but the one who knew
What lay beyond Time's change.

Therefore, do not grieve for your loss,
For that would be a double death
For him who relies upon you
To cross the long barren stretch
Which lies between chaos and birth;
And when the evening light falls
On your greying hair and dimmed eyes,
And you feel sad and lonely,
Do not dread the lengthening shadows,
Only remember that you carry
With you all the gold of our true being
To a world where there is no dying.

So when a taller shade than mine
Looms at last over your house
To lead you across silent seas
Where I anxiously wait for your return,
Do not fear the long cold hand
And the hoary, darkening gaze
Which will descend upon your limbs;
Only think that it is I, with greater
Heart and timeless breath,
And calmly lock your earthly doors
And walk into the night without alarm
Towards the eternity of waiting arms.

OUR LOGICS ARE DIFFERENT

Our logics are different, I am no longer
A man; only a centre of responses, a mirror
Which reflects or moves, as an object
Impinging on your senses, drawing tears
And passing joys, a temple that you visit,
But no longer a maze of nerves and cells,
Cerebrations and feelings, revolving
Round a tired, much debased muscle,
Called the heart.

The doors are closed; we meet
In the court-yard, or wave to each other
From windows; we may even exchange
A fleeting touch of hands by the gate,
But we each walk alone, to rooms
Where our secrets are beyond the range
Of the other, in worlds of burnt-out blooms,
Round a tired, much debased muscle,
Called the heart.

What is 'the cause' of it all, why have flowers
Turned to rank weeds, and Hesperides
Into lands of swamps and barren deserts?
Where is the light of the radiant dawn
When we hailed the sun from the mountain,
High above forests and the smoke of cities,
In a world whose only shadow was that of the eagle,
And with a throbbing and much entranced muscle,
Called the heart?

YOU WILL ONLY BE

The world offers you perfumes and songs
Which you distractedly acknowledge from absence,
Dawn unfolds from night, your limbs
Wholly your own, yet unclaimed in dreams,
Close as skin, cold as the moon.

Stone statue, vexed divinity,
You accept with hollowed eyelids
Sighs and prayers and all the absurdity
Of receiving in an empyrean world
Witholding from you suffering and birth.

Yet, you will never live until you bleed
And draw breath from your wounds
Like St. Sebastian and Christ on their wood,
Or martyrs whose blood quenched the sands;
Life will only begin once you are torn
From the loam of bliss and darkness
By a whirlwind which will rive the roof
Of your sleep and haul you like a sere leaf
Round every dank dark tumulus
Where men decay under human grief.

You will only be, once you are reduced to tears,
Covered in ashes, kneeling in prayers,
Your body — a mat, your soul — an oblation
To a force or a faith greater than you are,
In a surrender which will be annihilation.
Only once you have been sieved by lightless waves,
Furrowed and dissolved into the salt
Which corrodes and creates, and once you have swept
From your memory your name and your pride,
And from your heart every other desire
But to give, then, and then only, will you live.

THE HEART

They used to tell me, and I believed it, that
If it ached long enough the heart would break,
And then one would go through life like a husk
In the wind, hollow, carefree, unmindful
Of falls, wedding bells and funerary palls.
But this is not true; grief and gall
Never end, they live as long as the cells
And the heart sends blood through the veins.
You may believe that the huge pessimism
Of your youth and all its green longings
Have been swept away by the tides of years,
You may think you know that every plant
Can only bring forth its earthly fruit
And that the Hesperides can never live again;
Or there may be such silt in your breast,
Such sorrows in your world of shrunken shores
That you may feel that no rosy dawn
Or ink-blue sky, no sound or sight
Could ever awaken your embalmed heart!

You are mistaken; the beast only pretends
To be asleep, crouching low for a better spring,
Sharpening its claws on the bark of years,
Waiting by a choice glade where the golden
Gazelle or the mythical unicorn may come.
Then a sudden leap, and all is again
Involved in struggle; head sore, throat
Clutched by claws, eyes hynotized
By what they are trying to avoid,
The mind distraught, the body withdrawn
From the world, suspended in the void,
Its roots, cells, leaves and fruit
Being nothing but the waiting for being —
A silent symphony of annihilated sounds,
Or the fast-dying light of an extinct star
In the swift-crowding, infinite night.

SPRING

When on a warm spring morning
I see all around me trees
Clad in their rich blossoms,
And breathe the intoxicating scent
Of sensuous, gestating earth,
The blade of spent years stabs
My heart with a sudden wound
Which dissolves all dreams
Into cold, underground streams.

What's the use of fever in a brow
Which will soon be no more
Than a bowl of loam; why sorrows
And fleeting joys in a heart
Which so soon returns to earth?
What remains of men's exertions,
Even those which create monuments
And deeds that span centuries?
What are men's lasting joys?

Nobody has ever numbered them,
For nobody has ever returned
To tell those he loved and missed,
That the grave was a cosy place.
Kings and commoners, all leave
This short, sorrowful life
With sweating brow and writhing face,
For they all know what they lose
But they know not what they'll gain.

What remains of a man?
'A handful of dust to stop a hole'!
Perhaps, yet barely enough to fill
A heart, unless it be of a quality

So rare as to burn throughout history.
Life ceaselessly flows, like a stream
Along new shores, and what it carries,
It dissolves or drowns into its waves
Intent upon the roar of the ocean.

PRAYER

Oh God of mercy, look with forgiveness
Upon man's falls, misdeeds and pain,
The result of the unhealed dizziness
Which harrows him since his loss of Eden;

Guide him when, blind as a bat
In the dazzling light of your thought,
He only sees the boundless plain
Of the first dawn and the translucent trees

Of the unwounded world where movement
Was still, and where all lived in the freedom
Of dreams; sustain him
When, with terror and aching heart,

He longs for your thunderous absence
Which so stuns his mind that, restless,
He rolls through this world of dust
And sorrows, the toy of endless tides,

Praying, hoping that after aeons
Of darkness, shipwrecks and wrenched limbs,
After bitter salt and flaying winds,
He may reach, at last, the white of your shores.

IT'S TIME

It's time, it's time to stop at last
And to cast a backward glance before darkness
Falls and dissolves for ever
Our paradoxical plans and fevers,
Our dreams in palaces built on waves
And our sleep over gaping graves.

Faint light and widening shadows
Loom on the darkening summit; trees
Have long disappeared, and the grass
Is sparse and bleached like hair
In old age when the blood's frozen flow
Feeds slowly the stiffening limbs.

We are near the end of the journey,
The last stage before the cloister of silence
Where all tumult and human rage
Come to rest like sere leaves or snow
Into worlds of vaulted skies and peace,
Till the trumpet's shattering kiss.

So, before watery dreams and winds
Disperse us through and over the earth
Into anguished thoughts and longings
Which will last through Time's length,
Let me beg you to have no anxiety
Of oblivion from my dissolved memory,

Let me assure you that love
Is a fluid garment which is never cut
To a single shape, for it has to fit
All forms, from stone to foam;
Which is the best, no one can prove,
All I know is that it should bear your name.

DREAM

I dreamt of a girl with emerald eyes,
With lips saltier than sea waves
And arms like promontories of wind —
Swept rocks where I would lie
Until dawn arose from dark caves
And the deep surges of the mind.

I dreamt of a voice soft as the murmur
Of a mountain stream brushing the face
Of black rocks, or teasing leaves and grass
In its headlong rush to green pools
Where silvery, speckled trouts flicker
Or stand still like hunting hawks.

And all I found was a woman
Who had everything any other woman has,
Not more, nor less, and below the surface
Of paint, powder and padded bosom
Enough flaws to put Dante off his tale,
Cure him of love and drive him to Hell;

As for softness of temper, love
In every glance, languorous eyes,
Rapturous embraces sweet beyond belief,
Iseult's love on the edge of the grave
Or long hosannahs of fulfilled desires —
These are only dreams to feed men's grief.

Men should know better and never confuse
The living woman with the food of love
Or the poet's dream. Absence and the Muse
May turn a shrill-voiced shrew into a loving dove,
A flat shape into a moon-globed figure,
But love should never be wedded to nature.

THEY SAY

They say: 'You are a poet, so you need not
The real; pure honey is what you eat,
Nectar, not coarse wine, is what you drink,
And you can draw warmth from rock.'

They dismiss you as they dismiss a beggar
On a cold wintry night: 'He is a comedian
And he has in his garret, we feel sure,
As big a load of gold as on a Spanish galleon.'

Thus they enjoy their feasts with the contentment
Of men who are 'too wise to be made fools',
And who will let any beggar who pays no rent
Die, 'since he does not live according to the rules'.

Poets for them are beggars or nightingales
Who sing, but need no earthly food
And least of all a roof above their heads,
For they have their dreams, whatever the gales.

They need not be clad, they are not used to it,
They are ethereal, they hardly dwell on earth,
And since they neither make bread nor split atoms,
Why provide them with food and home?

Once upon a time they were needed
To entertain and to enthuse warriors into battles
Or to sing songs to their wives, bored
When their men were away at jousts or crusades.

Now men have greyhound and horse races,
Football matches, tennis and television,
And all that is needed is just one single versifier
To scribble mankind's epitaph after the final explosion.

THE WISDOM OF LIME

Oh, the sadness of hours lost in mental agony,
The chaos, the heart-rending grief of wine
Turned to vinegar through drops of acid words
More bitter than gall in the crucible of memory;
The harsh, gruelling thought that nothing of earth
Endures, that crystal splits and gold stains,
That roses born at dawn die with the night
And that days begun in joy ever end in pain!
Oh, to withdraw from life into the white of dreams,
Deep down in a room remote from noise and crowds,
The heart safely embalmed in a high pyramid
Secluded from men's eyes, severed from arteries and veins!
And tideless, sunless, byond the vagaries of time,
To sip slowly silence and the wisdom of lime!

AUTUMN

Now is the time when leaves turn
Brown or gold like dried-up blood,
And whirling hither and thither, fall
And join the heaps of simmering moulds
Where slender stem and sweet green
Melt into dark, singing decomposition;

Only the wood remains, stripped bare,
Shorn of spring and summer growth
Now silting slowly into the solacing earth
Or consumed into ashes with which the wind
Draws in the sky the image of the rose
Which endlessly rises from decay and dust.

HOME

Home is the familiar sounds
Beyond storms and rough seas,
The friendly bark, the wind
In the oak tree, the hurdles

Overcome, the scent of lotus
Drowned in the acrid smell
Of rustic smoke, and sirens
Lost on their drifting isles,

Home is what awaits us, the goal
Of the journey, the end of the ways,
The ashes, the boards, the clay walls
Where all salt returns to the well.

STRANGE MEETING

I suddenly fell into a dark pool
And deep down, beyond the shimmering wash
Of waves, I caught a glimpse of the golden
City I had long dreamt of,
It bore your name, and I did not know it.
Every street had a statue with your face,
Every window bled with the slit
Pomegranate of your lips and every house,
Every tree was a complex of lines,
Flailing the air in a bewildering world
Caught in the grip of frozen silence.
Only the dark waves of your eyes
Flowed on, carrying on their surf
White-maned horses and a tide
Which swept the sands and left
In its wake a world of uprooted hopes
Which could only be brought to life
By a forever mourned, forever lost face.

TO A GROUNDED SAILOR

What shores, or whores, cerulean-eyed,
White-sanded, white-limbed, peppered
With pines and shady spots to nap
Away the randy noon, have you visited?

How many dreams or babes, water-born,
Water-logged, have been drowned and lost
In seasonal or summery commerce
Between palmy islands and sandy coves!

How often did you find the north-west passage
To the still, hoary Pole, where all is silence,
Or the warm currents towards Hesperides
Of golden apples and scented leaves?

How often did you fall into the great well
Of sleep with crowns of red berries
Round your head, and with your sea-shell ears
Ringing with the cooing of doves and sirens' songs?

Ah, there was the life for the sea-legged sailor!
While now your woolly knees can only wobble
And buckle under the somersaults of the long ribs,
Compelling you to lie hump-backed in wistful
Corners, gazing at the mane of the passion-tossed sea,

Now the mast is stowed away into a shed,
The sails folded, the engine thrown to the wind,
And the fair-limbed boat is a hump of boards,
Sand-stained, sun-bleached, dream-drowned,
A shell echoing the roar of the receding ocean!

PIETA

Pride was the sin the ancients never forgave,
Their jealous gods destroyed any who dared
To forget the distance between gods and men;
Ilion was burnt to ashes for having listened
To the cunning song of Venus; Arachne
The weaver was turned into a spider,
And Niobe into rock shedding endless tears.

Fears and tears, all for private sorrows!
One woman alone mourns for the grief of men,
It is the one who in the grey dawn
Of the longest night, at the foot of the cross
Which rises from man's heart to Heaven,
Holds upon her knees the mangled body
Of the beloved Son who lived and died
To show men that they are never alone,
That a fatherly care ever watches their steps,
That cross and spear must be endured,
And that no night is without His light.

Mother of Life, womb of all men,
Source of all joys and pains,
Eternal Pieta transfixed by sorrows,
Condemned to watch to the end of time
Some of her sons nail onto crosses
The best of themselves, the Christs for whom
Her greatest died and will die endlessly
Until the stillness of the last human cell.

CHRISTMAS DAY

Can we, on this day of songs and chiming bells,
Fail to see, beyond the cherub's smile
And the mother's love-illumined face,
The swelling tears and the stalking cross?

Can we forget, if we believe the fable,
That because of ours and Adam's folly
This child, this Son of God,
Was only born to bleed upon a tree?

Can we ignore the grief of a woman
Who, because of Eve and the pity of the fall,
Wove in her womb the bitter gall
And the salt which filled her wounds?

Can we drown in mirth our guilt,
And ignore the doom He was born for?
Can we, who caused sorrow and hanging,
Ever welcome sacrifice with song?

Let children rejoice, they are pure as fire,
And let those who wish, wear their shirts
Of sin till the last hour of their pyre,
But let them forsake the tiger-thought

That, be it Christ, soldier, sailor or airman,
Be it now, tomorrow or twenty centuries ago,
In Eastern lands or on the banks of Jordan,
Joy can be bought with someone's blood or sorrow.

MAZEPPA'S RIDE

What's this absurd paradox,
This blind animal tied to a corpse
Whose slow-sifting decay
Pervades his blood and bones
Till in the end the dying and the dead
Sleep in the same clay bed?

Where is he from, what's the aim
Of his wild, headlong race,
Spurred by his haunting burden,
Trying in vain to shake his yoke,
Desperate to annihilate distance
And to bury fear into the dark?

Is he Prometheus tied upon his rock,
Burning in his sorrow, winnowed
By hovering wings, his vision widened
To the infinite by the piercing beak
Which, in a shower of red, lifts him
To the height where his Maker lives?

Is he Hercules consumed by fire,
Dissolved into the sap of vernal births,
Or is he Christ, worm-nailed to his cross,
Wantonly stretched from East to West,
His Adam's feet rooted in the earth,
His blood streaming up to the stars?

He is man obsessed by memories of light,
He is the uncrowned king hunted
By slaves through groves, where each shade
Hides the mediating blade, he is
The only one in an indifferent universe
Who is haunted by death and his lost innocence.

PRAYER

Oh God, give me the force to pray with heart
Split by waking blade and eyes agape
To mounting gales and closing gates,
Give me the strength to bear,
Along the tense, taut strings
Of fading mind and in-drawn breath,
The wind which from Heaven brings
The melody which dissolves and raises
The soul from these alien shores of tumult
To the light and white where no-thing
Breathes or bleeds, where all there is
Is unheard music beyond ears,
And movement stilled beyond wounds,
A no-place where all is and wants to be,
For only there are all things in joy,
Complete beyond Time's stress,
Wrapped up into whiter than white,
And burning in a tempest of light
Which transfixes all knowing into darkness.

ANSWER

Bound to life by five senses,
Bleeding through five wounds,
Dreaming of a world where truth
Lives beyond nails and spear,
Forsake what cannot be held,
Surrender what cannot be owned,
Welcome the thrust in the breast,
And closing the eyes upon all I's,
Drop blind into an endless fall
Which He who sees all
Might turn into a flight
To the never-ending dawn.

LAZARUS

A lid upon his head, in his head,
Dreaming of Eden among the dead,
His heart ground by the grip of Time,
His eyes lost in absence and night
His bones heavy with the weight of lime,
His skin brushed past by feathers and fins
Of prehistoric animals with which he lived,
He waited for the footfalls of the dove
And the words which, in a choir of light,
Would lift the lid weighing upon the world.

From his prison of earth and his heart,
His long lean limbs locked by Adam's chains
Longing for the caravans fading in the dust
And the voice of sirens in the diluvial rains,
He waited for Dawn to crow the day born
To turn grief-laden Time into lasting gold,
And to redeem the white grace of years
When Man could hear the music which filled
The air before the fall of the morning star.

How long did he wait? Nobody knows,
Nobody can tell.
For time, which furrows faces into folds
And kneads hearts and eyes into clay,
Is an unredeemable ghost which rises and falls
With the blood's uncharted tides and remains
Changing and the same, the eternal shadow
Of the source whence it came.

With a lid on his head and the weight of lime
In his sorrow-laden heart, he slept
Until a voice purer than the first dawn,
Stronger than the one which brought down

Jericho's walls, shook the web of years
And tore open the serpent-skin of woes
And the night which shut from men's eyes
The longed-for light of the undying star.

WHAT MATTERS

What matters if rivers are deep
And woods dark and full of knives?
I would face again — the dew-laden sleep
Of childhood, the aches in the green leaves,
The spring pyres on hills at falling night
Burning the blood, singeing the heart
Till only sorrow remains to fill the dreams
Of a tired head slowly bending to the grave.

I would gladly return to earth's marshes
Where men, like fish or flies, spawn
And crawl over one another with cries
Of anger or bliss; I would search again
For lost shores and light from the skies,
Kneel again in prayer, endure disdain
With the faith that there is in man's plight
A force which can illumine his night.

I would consent to face again the retches
Of the dying and the struggle in marshes
Where all senses live beyond clocks
Ticking the hours, summoning shapes to cross
The horned gate of sighs and shrieks,
For I know that in spite of blindness,
Suffering and death, man knows joys
Which bring song to the shores of silence.

IN MID AIR

See how the horseman frozen in mid air
Feels for the earth which he will never reach,
See how the heart's soft beats unfold
The lethal dross which clogs the blood.

Each wave of red flood carries death with it,
Each tide shatters the decaying walls,
The shuttling heart weaves the net
Which folds its wings into a final fall.

Heavenly hours or harrowing moments,
Each grinds the dust which chokes the heart,
Honey's sweetness hides the bee's sting,
The shadow of death lurks in everything.

THREE SONGS

I GENTLE BOAT

Gentle boat with the white sails,
Where will you take me,
Gentle bird by the waterfall,
What are you saying to me?
Shall we go to the golden East
And to the isle of the blest
Where lamb and tiger
Free from hatred and fear
Walk through the woods
In primal brotherhood?
Or shall we go to the land of sorrow
Where fruits wither on the bough
And care furrows every brow?
Oh tell me, tell me, oh,
Little bird, where shall I go?

II ONCE I LOVED

Once I loved a woman fair,
Fair as was ever known,
But oh! that I had never met her,
For she was a faithless one!

My heart could sing now and ever
How dear she was to me,
But what's the use of thinking of her
And of a love that will never be?

Could I but speak, I would tell you
Of all the grief she brought to me,
But I can only sigh in sorrow
For a love that will never be.

III WAITING

I sit by the window
Watching the waves,
Counting the leaves
While the wind blows;

So sad am I when nights
Follow days, and days
Follow nights, that
I can only sigh and pray;

I wait for white sails
To bring you over the sea —
Oh may God's sweet angels
Guide my love back to me;

For if you were never to return,
I know my heart would break,
And I would become a nun
Wearing nothing but black.

TO A CHILD ASLEEP

Spelled to sleep from fabulous leaves,
Dropped deep down beyond the spying senses,
Grope by your inner light through caves,
Magic strands or glass palaces;

Whether in the signless wastes of the finned world
Or caught in the spinning wheels of the stars,
Move through timelessness, sowing the hours
As Tom Thumb pebbles in his uncharted wood.

May the sweet herbs of night feed
Your innocence and candid beliefs
That you live and move in a world of friends
Where falls and fictions are your only griefs;

May you never be scared into losing the faith
That you can teach stars to sing, or fashion
All things by the command of your mouth!
May you long be spared the chains of reason,

Long may you dwell in spacious dreams
Which turn the earth into a magic lantern
And Heaven and Hell into the painted slides
Which on the secret screen vision unfolds!

Long may you keep your palaces bright
And your fairies alive, long may you mock
The illusion of a world spanned by the senses,
And, later in life, whenever lost, remember Blake.

DANCERS' DREAM

Spring blossoms burn like candles
In the cold air full of stars;
Under them, two phantasmic dancers
Caught in the glare of night
Dance upon the mind's stage
The arabesque of an obsessing urge,

Limbs wrapped in liquid fire,
They move towards each other
In a lunar world of wild roses,
Oblivious of creation's cross purpose,
Desperate to bury into the dark
The metaphor which holds them apart,

But Time who keeps a banker's eye
On all things and everyone's account,
In a world of dissembling skies,
Denies these dancers' overdraft
And quickly turns the page of light
And puts an end to bankrupt night.

ISLAND-BORN

Island-born, sea-spawned,
The sea is the mirror
Where I learnt all I can remember;
As soon as my eyes could focus
On the horizon, I stood transfixed
By sails or smoke drawing in the sky
Paintings of unknown lands.

Later on, dazzled by magic leaves,
All ships carried Helen and Paris,
Aeneas fleeing Dido, or Columbus

Searching for his truth — the Indies,
Beyond tall steeples and cathedral waves,
To the ultimate shore of no return;
How often have I watched from my window
This feathered shape flying westward,
Past redeeming whirls of blue flames
Towards golden sands and silence!

Oh my island of craggy rocks
And green-covered slopes
Lulled by the whispering sea
Enfolding you in her arms!
What longings, what dreams
You must once have raised
In the lonely head of a fallen eagle —
Your son, pinned like an owl
To the barn door of an Atlantic rock,
Waiting for death to lift him
On her wings and bring him home!

Oh to lie dazed on your scorching rocks,
Teased by the song of cicadas at noon,
To watch the golden locks of wheat
Sway in the breeze and the blazing sun,
Or the moon turn the proud oak
Into a god-carved silver head!
Oh my island, burnt out by summer heat,
Drunk under the weight of fruit,
When, oh when shall I see again
Your wild butterflies and shimmering light,
When shall I hear again
The organ music of your pine-trees,
And when will your rosy dawn
Rub its scented nose at my window?

DESERTED VILLAGE

An air of ancestral doom hangs
Over this place; olive trees like hawks
Claw the rocky chest of the earth,
Seeking to deny the giant's strength.

Motley-skinned lizards scurry in holes
And the tingling bells of goats pierce
The veil of silence which swiftly falls
From the hills to these darkening slopes.

On either side of the road, the remains
Of a few houses, a communal oven
Strewn with shards and a derelict garden
Spell out the misdeeds of civilization.

Propped against these torn, roofless walls,
A chestnut tree preens its glistening leaves;
At its feet, a stream uncoils its limbs
Over the dark snout of crouching rocks.

On the floor of one of these ghostly houses
The skeleton of a long-dead goat
Sprawls like a heraldic painting
On the walls of a primitive cave,

By its side a Greek god — Dionysos —
Sadly sings of centuries past
And slowly walks in the greying light
Towards the blue oblivion of night.

FILITOSA

It is the end of the day; the sun
Slowly hauls his golden nets
Over tree-tops, green slopes
And the lingering gaze of glaucous pools.

Caught in the mesh of this golden trail,
A stone statue, rectangular from shoulder
To toe, stands still amid boulders,
Guarding the peace of these lonely hills.

Lengthwise sword and diagonal dagger,
Crowned by a flat, hairy head,
Compose the proud bearing of the warrior
Who stands on guard over his dead;

Yonder tumulus rising behind him
Is the place where they lie buried
Or burnt, under strangely carved stones,
In the age-long rest where they were laid.

Beyond this mound, across a river,
Four knights of different size
Lined up shoulder to shoulder
Indifferent to moon — or sun-rise,

Watch over the remains of their brethren —
Our ancestors who twenty thousand years ago
Squabbled, laughed, lived and died
With joys and fears which are ours also.

Dusk is falling over the wounded earth,
And from this millenary mound, whispering bones
And flowing blood ceaselessly proclaim the truth
That creation is intent upon stone.

(Filitosa is a place in the South-West of Corsica, where menhirs, statues and burial mounds have recently been unearthed.)

DISTANT VALLEY

The language I understand best
Is that of leaves muttering dissent
Or whispering advice and support
Whenever I need it most.

The sound that sinks deepest
In memory's pool and echoes
Down the years, back to curly locks
And bare feet on burning earth,

Is that of water leaping from stone
To stone, glistening over green scales,
Winking, whistling heavenly tunes
And filling with voices the living vale.

The dance that moves me most
Is that of pine-needles tossed by the wind,
Gracefully whirling green limbs
Reflecting the light of shimmering pools.

The sight I love best is the sun
Majestically enthroned on a mountain range
Showering down its white wisdom
With prodigal, indifferent hands.

In this brimming light all stands still,
The senses fade away from the mind,
Back to limpid dawns filled with birds
Calling each to each from the hills,

Until the sudden fall of a leaf
Stills the heart to stone
With the thought that all that ripens
Must fall to dark, waiting earth.

HOMEWARD

What is it that turns my thoughts
Toward you my surf-laced island
With white-headed mountain tops
And winding ribbons of glittering sand?

Why is it that before, I could only dream
Of maps, compasses and the way ahead,
Never looking back at the receding seas
Or at crying gulls flying landwards?

What mysterious voice calls me home
From dark woodlands and sea-caves,
What force ceaselessly urges me on
To retrace my steps over the waves?

Is it the slanting sun and fading light,
Is it the church bells ringing evensong,
Or have the visions which filled my mind
Fled like migrating birds in autumn?

What is home, where is home?
Is it my island with scented shrubs,
Or golden Pythagoras's uncharted isle
To which we all sail without return?

NOON-DAY SUN

The noon-day sun fills the valley
And drives birds and animals to sleep
In the brooding silence of the brushwood;
A golden hawk hangs from the blue,
Above the still, shimmering stream;
Nothing moves except the human cells

Endlessly rolling towards the waiting sea,
While pinned to memory's banks, the mind
Watches with mounting sorrow
The fading light and deepening furrows.

Water flows but does not alter,
It is the same everywhere;
Flower or snow covered, the earth,
Indifferent whore, gives or receives
With a blank face; man alone —
A cage filled with fleeing birds —
Grieves at their loss and ever sees,
Beyond blossom and singing leaves,
The bed of clay which for him waits.

Heavenly music, hallowed hours
Which sometimes dispel the dark
And give tongue to singing oaks,
Cannot hide the haunting hum
Of gestating earth and sighing grass
And the rattle of bones battered by rain
Or tossed about by playing dogs.

ASCO

The giant's brow broods upon its solitude
Watching, with disdain, pigmy pines
Forward bent, trying in vain to crawl
Along its furrowed chest to its forehead;

At its knees, a river roars in anger
And dances and leaps from rock to rock
To show that if it can't stand on air
It has nimble feet, speech and no roots.

Mountains are tied by the waist to the earth,
Trees are held down by giant hands
And they shake in vain their angry heads
As powerless as Samson at Delilah's feet.

Water mocks them both with its foam,
Its headlong tumbles and varied songs,
Its merry-go-round across lands and oceans
Which will last the whole earth long.

On its banks, man, untied the while,
Yet earth-bound — a seeming of presence,
A metaphor caught in falls and pools —
Longs for roots and the death of conscience.

CORSICA

A landscape which breaks the heart
And a child in a world of ghosts
Trying to grasp with a wrinkled hand
A wistful star in the pale blue sky.

Scented shrubs, trees straight as rods
And among them, green years and the ache
Of receding dreams flowing back
To griefless dawns of singing woods.

Under the sun when it flails the plain
In the rage of summer, in the shade of a tree,
By the white-laced aquamarine sea,
Or along dusty roads sizzling in the rain,

Always the same mutation of man into child,
King of the winged and leafy world,
Dancing in the glory of his newly-born days
And stabbed to the heart by the thought of spent year

WHEN NIGHT FALLS

When night falls upon my eyes
And folds away for time's length
My aimless arms still intent
Upon the shadow of your shape,

Then my mind will ache no more
Nor dread the years wasted away
Waiting in vain for your return
And the harvest gold of autumn,

Then stillness will heal all wounds,
And whatever form you take,
Whether you live in a star
Or join the endless fall of black suns,

I shall know you, when stone you roll
By my side, or rain you fall
On the grass where I shall lie
Listening for sounds of known sighs.

If you live on leaves or wings,
I shall be the wind of the solar seas
Bringing to you memories of spring
And songs from earthly skies,

Trees will rustle with your voice,
Weeping grass will shed your tears,
Water will echo the sound of your steps
And every line compose your face,

Then fear shall be no more,
For freed from eyes and hands
I shall find and see you everywhere,
And nameless we shall live
Beyond Time and shifting sands.

SPIDERS

A spider propels itself in space,
Slowly sliding up to the green lobes
Of chestnut leaves, the palace
Where it weaves its princely robes;

Another descends the ladder of Heaven,
A small brown patch, swinging
On nothing, till it alights on the green
Spire of a cathedral pine.

Far away, in the distance, the red eye
Of the sun enfolds in its glowing gaze
The silvery limbs of a birch tree
Shaking its locks in a shower of gold.

I sit still, watching sun and sky
Conjure up sleep upon the earth,
And caught in unease, I wonder why
I too could not walk on air,

I wonder what keeps me earthbound!
Is it the weight of matter, the lack
Of a solid, yet unbreakable thread,
Or the wings which lifted Jacob?

I wonder why a spider knows
its way to Heaven, and I don't;
I wonder what is the I that dreams
And the flesh that ties it to earth,

I wonder and keep on wondering
While the blue, thickening air
Slowly hushes all whisperings
And stills the leaves to a shudder,

Until all dreams and longings sink
Into a metaphysic of silence,
And the lengthening shadow of trees
And a faint haze soon close the book,

Leaving all questions unanswered.

THE INTRUDER

The water, liquid diamond, leaps
From stone to stone; on its bank, marigolds
Spill their scent over a motley mosaic
Reflecting the changing schemes of light.

A lark, aloft in the blue,
Pours down the gratuity of its song
On the lap of carefree mother nature —
Closed circle of earth and sky.

Light flows down from indifferent Heaven,
Water follows the laws of its density,
And a clump of trees set in green
Composes a picture of Edenic serenity;

Alone, the remains of a fire stain the sand,
Disclosing the incinerated human fact;
Nothing but the self intrudes
Upon the diamond of non-being.

With it, the worm in the fruit —
Man — maker of meaning and death,
Stills the song in the lark's throat,
Turns water to tears and music to sighs.

What remains? A broken mirror,
A collage-picture made to tell
A tale gratuitously imposed upon nature
By man ever intent on having his will!

TRY AS I MAY

Try as I may I can never replace
With words or works your absent face;
Walking the streets, watching falling leaves,
Following dreams on the wings of birds,
Or listening to sparrows squabbling on eaves,
I can never succeed in exorcising the ghost
Whose footsteps echo in my heart,
Or forget the silence of your voice.

All things partake of you, and while I converse
With you, the words take your place,
Become you, and I become you also,
King of endless moments, oblivious
Of harrowing Time and gnawing winds,
Until a stone slips from under my foot,
And I stumble once more into a dark hole,
Face to face with my naked self.

WOULDN'T YOU

Wouldn't you like to tear mountains apart
And reach the vale of unquenched fires
Or heave the hawsers and let the boat
Ride the waves towards obsessing horizons!

Wouldn't you like to shake off all ties,
To shut off your ears to sounds and calls
And wildly plunge into rising seas
To be rolled away to unknown landfalls!

Wouldn't you like the hush of a desert wind
Across your face, drying up your tears,
Burning your thoughts, scorching your limbs
With astral music to drown all fears!

You need not answer! Your eyes unfold
The ebb and flow of brooding storms,
Your hands carve worlds on air,
And your lips quiver in aching prayer.

Yet in the dark of your head, a light
Flickers like a beam over rough seas
And warns you of shipwrecks and the night
Which its fading out would let loose,

So, with your heart in your hands
You stumble on through mounting shadows,
Your limbs flailed by burning winds
Caught in the tides of unredeemed sorrow.

NIGHT

Night falls, the light recedes
Over the sinuous sea;
The moon rises, trailing its red
Gauze over the orange-fringed waves,
The owl stands still in the oak-tree
Waiting to make sure that his enemy —
The sun — is safely asleep in his cave.

Soon, the croaking of frogs in watery leaves
Sweeps out of the sky all human cries;
All things fade, and turn into shades
Slow-rising sap and haunted silence.

Only the moon remains,
Tired bald pate,
Hollow, blind eye,
Wandering mournfully
Across the plains
Of the sky.

A SILENT FIRE

Thus the earth which will receive you
Is already torn open by Time's plough
And the ice which will enfold you
Is creeping along the walls of your cells.

Unseen by you moves the black banner
Which sweeps over trees and stones
And turns the green and gold of summer
Into the grey ashes of unborn dawns.

A silent fire is consuming your days
Until you are nothing but smouldering embers —
A seeming of living, which black wings,
Brushing past, will disperse to the winds.

YOU ARE BEING FOLLOWED

A mangy dog paws the air
Rubbing his back on the grass
To shake a flea or allay an itch;
An old woman shudders on a bench,
A blackbird sways back and forth
Hauling up an unwilling worm,
While green leaves wave you by
On your indifferent road.

You are being followed, wherever you go;
When you sleep, she lies by your side
Until the fateful dawn
When she will rise and leave you behind;
When you walk, she sidles by you
More faithful than your shadow
Until the day when she will loosen

Your limbs or cut your sinews,
And you will drop to the ground.

A dog feels his fleas and his needs
But does not know that he is followed;
A beetle blunders across your path
Unmindful of your death-carrying foot;
Man alone nurses this shadow
In his heart and this light in his skull.

Prospero's magic was of no avail to him,
Every third thought became his grave
Until his thought and his grave were one.

WHAT'S THE USE?

What's the use of shouting against the roar
Of the ocean or moaning against the wind
Which sweeps on from distant shores
And grinds all fears in the mill of the mind?

Nothing can be altered by our cries,
The great Deities will not bend their heads,
And the wide-eyed birds which ply the sky
Will not be halted in their wild races,

The tides will not cease to sieve
In their to-and-fro the pebbles of the shore,
The trees will shed no leaves
And the dead will not break their slumber,

Nothing that man does can stop
The sad song of the chained sea
Which raves and rails with its waves
At the stillness of the enfolding rocks.

WHY ARE WE HERE?

The world's weight may lie still
In the palm of the hand, the winds
May drop, the sails
Slacken, but not the questing mind.

On and on it goes, asking why we are here,
What purpose we are meant to fulfil
And what sorrow or shame we must endure
Before we reach the other side of the hill.

Wherever we turn, to lofty mountains,
Plains, lakes, rolling waters
Or voices long-stilled under stone,
We always get the same answer;

Christ got His own upon the cross,
Our fast-decaying flesh unfolds
The scroll where at the end it lies,
To be finally read with closed eyes;

We move from far away, beyond blood,
Bones, wombs or friendly smiles,
Out of a merry dance of molecules
Into the weightless sleep of the infinite.

NOT THE YEARS

Not the years but death alone
Can still the senses of the poet,
And there lie the salt of regret
And the source of sighs and dreams.

How sad when caught in the wind
Of spring, the sails suddenly fall
Leaving the boat stone-still,
Gasping for the wide, rolling horizon!

How lovingly the trees bend their heads
And stretch their branches and leaves
Over this swiftly passing shadow
Haunted by the light of summer eves!

Oh the rage of a wild bird
Longing for seas and high mountains
Locked in a cage of fragile bones
With a more and more rarefied air!

Its eyes still go on scanning the horizon
Continuously drawing across the sky
The primal geometry of its origins —
The shortest line between prey and eye;

But now, it's all eyes and no prey,
The iron bars have come closer,
The roof's rafters are lower
And the horizon looms grey, like clay.

ALL THAT WE ARE

All that we are is the result of our thoughts,
Said the Buddha under his bo-tree,
Yet, in spite of that, all Penelope's efforts
Could not wean Ulysses from the rival sea.

What are thoughts which cannot turn to deeds?
A piercing flame, a gnawing pain,
A rending claw and grinding wind
Causing deeper furrows than sea or rain.

GRIEF

Grief in art must be cleansed
From the tensions and sorrows of the heart;
Its component parts must be hauled
From the sea of memory and fused
By the cool, unsingeing fire of the mind
Which lives in a world of its own
Free from tears, will and emotions.

Grief must surge from uncharted depths,
Winged up by the urge to light,
Towards imagined, living shapes —
Timeless incandescences of foam
On the ever-changing ocean of Time;

Grief is not personal, it comes from Adam —
God's tear on the hot crust of the earth
Where the liquid sky mirrored his solitude
Until Eve turned the mirror into a dark wood,

And ever since, the progeny of Abel and Cain
And the animals which Time has bred
Have blundered on, carrying in their hearts
The original grief of Adam's pain —

That of being born, and of knowing
That men can only think of grief
By going back to the first falling leaf
Which shook Adam from his green sleep.

I CANNOT COMPARE YOU

I cannot compare you to this or that,
Make a cosmic map out of your shape,
And sing the discovery of its hills and coves
As if I were Columbus or a modern astronaut;

I cannot; actions need no words,
And words and thoughts are private
And cannot be used to construct
Exhibits for others to deny or applaud.

Our love is its own infinite end
Excluding listeners or sight-seers;
The world only needs to know, if it cares,
That you can turn darkness into light,

That like a river intent upon the ocean,
Your clear waters, knowing no marshlands
Or weed-ridden banks, move forward
Life-giving, reflecting Heaven,

That, like some Greek statues, you've no hands
To take from others; only a centre filled
With golden substance, freely offered
To transfigure all — this world, and beyond.

THE SNOWMAN

The snowman in the garden
Which yesterday was six feet tall
Is today down to ground level
And about to fade under the earth.

Time and the sun have shrunk him
To the fragment which will sleep
In the loam, or ceaselessly ride
The transparent horses of the moon.

Like snow in the sun, the blood
Thickens and passes from gold to lead
Which suddenly stiffens the knee
And removes the rider from the horse,

But the silent, shadow race continues;
Unshod, unbridled, tireless horses
Gallop across the fields of the earth,
Led by the undying horseman — Death!

A WALK IN THE PARK

Cerulean blue strewn with white scarves
Tossed by the wind, autumn colours —
Russet and green and falling leaves —
The nearby pond shimmers in the sun.

The earth exudes heat after the storm
And out of the haze, two penguin nuns
Step out in time, towards Heaven
Which nods at them right above the green.

A thrush baptises himself in the joy
Of a puddle; head down, tail up,
The world is a shower of diamonds
And a reel round the axle of his bill.

In this scene, man, outsider and recorder,
Ignored by all, yet holding all in his mind,
Wonders how long it will be before painter
And picture are one and the same thing.

SLANTING SUN

Trees full of shapes,
Earth full of sounds,
Blue sky — gauze on skin
And across haunting eyes;
Why this music, these colours
And these all-embracing gossamers!

Whom do they want to delay,
Enchant or imprison
In this dying, slanting sun
Pouring its golden sadness
Over the green shawls of trees
And the brooding silent stones?

Yet, do they really care?
Is not this the anguished cry
Of the heart stabbed with sorrow
At the perennial joy of trees,
The ageless face of mountains
And the whispers of waiting stones!

For soon, trees show their bare bones,
Crystal streams turn soggy brown,
Rocks take the shape of mausoleums
And the light fades in a widening grin.

SUN AND SEA

Scientists in their laboratories,
Astronomers in their dark chambers,
All wholly aseptic, dressed in white,
Inoculated against emotions and passions,
Washed clean from desires and volitions,
Masked, gloved, glass-caged,
Observe unmoved the faked pregnancies
Of the moon, the red tails of quasars,
And record, without a flutter in their pulse,
Facts, figures, concepts, hypotheses,
Called pure, immaculate knowledge,
In contrast with the emotion-soiled,
Heart-stained knowledge of the poet and the sage.

Archimedes had to plunge into his bath
To tumble to the truth that the bigger the rump
The stronger the push towards the light —
A strange contradiction between matter and spirit!
Newton cast a cold eye on a falling apple,
And deduced from it the law of gravitation;
But Dante had to be snubbed at the church door
And made to eat the bitter bread of exile,
Before he could wring from his Aeolian heart
The great song of the human condition.

Sun and sea, mind and heart
Are each barren, if kept apart;
The sun breathes and moves over the sea,
Which swells with desire and heaves
Her countless bosoms towards his thirst
And the burning embrace from which truth
And illumination are ceaselessly born.

Sun and sea are for ever locked
In a tangled rhythm of rises and falls;
The sea unfolds her vast, fecund depths
To the kiss of light and the pull of the heights,
And the two, rolled in the same wave, create life
And the divine truth which never divides
But always unites, and never allows the separation
Of music, or dancer, from the dance.

WHY

Why this ceaseless piling up of words
Upon words — Pelion upon Ossa,
Sisyphus's endless trek! To what end,
Above all, what causes this fever?

What world am I trying to reach
Or to forget, or is it both in one!
Am I trying to achieve forgetfulness
Or to protest against darkling oblivion?

Why write, why paint, if not to kill
Time and dredge up the truth
From deep down the dark well
Whence we came and where we return?

Why this itch that only ink can cool,
Why this urge to pin upon walls
The butterflies of the mind, or pour out,
On white, the hidden streams of the heart!

Rabbits would die if they couldn't grind
Their teeth against trees' bark or roots,
Poets would choke or burst like fruit
If they couldn't spill the lava of their minds.

Why is it so? Why do salmon return
To the waters of their birth, why do tigers
Kill, or glow-worms shine in the dark!
It's all part of the same mysterious order.

We are born and we have to die,
Whatever we may do; every autumn
Leaves turn to gold, and winter
Follows, and they moulder in the snow.

New leaves will grow, new men
Will be born, but that's no consolation
For what sleeps in the earth and never returns
Or lives, except in the mind of those who live on.

Is the pain we feel at falling leaves
The dark premonition of the dreaded fall
From the white-walled cities of life,
Through fold upon fold of primal shadows?

Perhaps, perhaps, for it is hard
To leave this world and face alone
The long sea-journey which divides
Light from darkness, the known from the unknown.

Is art man's cry against Death,
Are the translucent creations of the mind
The silvery lights which defy the dark
And, weightless, float in the wake of the earth!

In their caves, thousands of years ago,
Men pinned their dreams on rocks
And with them, denied space and the dark
And broke the fetters of fear and sorrows.

Since then, irrespective of climes, men
Have continued to catch haunting visions
In the meshes of mind and imagination
So as to keep at bay the crowding night.

TO T. S. ELIOT

You would not like me to mount a rostrum
And proclaim your virtues and talents;
Your gentle smile and wry wisdom
Would soon deflate such unwanted flights.

You wouldn't like me to strike attitudes,
To parade sorrow as a dark mirror
Reflecting your great, spent light,
Or use your loss to write dull odes.

All you might allow me to say, under protest,
Is that you, who were so cool and controlled
In your verse and in the web of your thought,
So perfectly master of the flow of your emotions,

Were also the most affectionate of men,
The most kind-hearted of friends —
A man whose humility and capacity to love
Were born from the obscure, illuminating night.

THOUGHTS BY T.S. ELIOT'S GRAVE

In my beginning is my end — that's certainty,
In my end is my beginning — there is doubt,
Except for those who stand on rock,
Like you, or the prisoner of Fotheringay.

For, this dark beginning is so different
From what we can think or know
That even those enfolded in Christ's arms
Tremble at the thought of the light
Which will blot out their senses

And wrench them out of their roots
Like whirling leaves in roaring winds,
To transform them into eternal song.
But how can the mind, how can the heart
Forsake without terror the scent of flowers,
The tides of the senses and the music of colours?

The dear lost friend on whose tombstone
I knelt today, had never such doubts;
Neither had Pascal, yet infinite space
Frightened him, infinitely small and frail,
Simply because the loss of identity,
The disintegration of the cells, frighten us all.

Christ in us, Christ around us,
Ever present, through life without end,
Strengthens us, comforts us, yet the cry
Which came to His lips in the half-lit garden
Comes also to ours in the bitter hour
That tears apart the music from the shell,
For the shell is also the music,
And we cannot bear the thought of being
Nothing but music in celestial spheres.

All attempts at consolation, all words
Are barren, fruitless, a mouthful of dust,
Every human explanation makes it worse,
Is less than useless, for it destroys
The nothingness of light and the music
In which, mindless, senseless, we truly are,
Without knowing who we are.

The picture of Christ as leader
Of hosts, warrior of holy causes,
Deprives me of Christ, diminishes
And darkens the great light holding together

Kings and beggars, vanquished and victors.
Christ is dazzling darkness, light
Of life and death, and no one can be praised
Because He chose to be born a Jew,
Or blamed because He died among them,
For it was a God-chosen birth, and death.

Are these thoughts heretical,
Which came to me, dear friend,
As I was kneeling in prayer,
Thinking of you, certain that if a spirit
Had refined itself into the readiness for God,
Had striven to shed all impurities
And to live by love and Christ's teaching,
It was yours!

FOR MARGARET

Oh, shall I ever pierce the secret
Of that innocent, silent stare,
When huddled up in crumpled sheets,
Your breath hovering on the edge of sleep,
Your blood suspended between water and stone,
Your shrunken body burnt into a living soul,
You looked and looked and with aching hands
Tried to utter words or thoughts welling
Up from the depths towards which you were falling!

What cold hand did you feel,
What wild light did you see
Which your silent tongue
Sought in vain to reveal?

Oh, how sad to watch your great spirit
Struggle against the closing gates
Of the frost-laden February night
And the gaping earth waiting for you!

And while Time had melted away the years
And reduced you to the innocence of the womb,
Once again a child in the cradle
Preparing for your last birth,
We watched you behind an armoury of lies,
Encouraging you to make plans
Which we knew would be still-born,
And every night when we left you alone,
The prey of the dark closing upon you,
We walked away in shame and guilt
At being unable to help you.

And now that the earth is lying upon you,
By night or by day, on mountains,
In forests or at sea, in aching spring
Or numbing winter, in dead silence,
Blinding rain or roaring winds,
I shall always hear your anguished whisper
And see everywhere your hurt stare.

THE TIME OF THE RISING SEA

Our world is no longer young, as in the days
Of Astarte, Buddha, Socrates or Christ;
It no longer dreams of new dawns
To light men's paths to Nirvana or Heaven;
All these dreams are dead, and what remains
Is the anaesthesia of sex, drink and drugs,
And beyond that, hollow night and silence.
There is only sand, and the noonday sun —
A burning glare without shadow or light.

Death is only a name, a sign on a clock,
No longer the narrow gate, or the rite
Of passage to perennial shores and true being.
Only those who know how to die and why they die
Know how to live and why they live.
Now, men obsessed by the fear of age and nothingness
Seek only the oblivion of the intoxicating present,
The rich are dead in life, cocooned in their wealth,
And like Tutankhamen will have themselves embalmed
To defeat Time; only the poor truly die
And will go on dying every day of their lives,

Cheated, lied to, used as cattle
To produce wealth and power for men
Who, by force or wiles, have stuck a yoke
On their necks and, with carrot or whip,
Guile them on or compel them to plough furrows
And sow new crops, from which will rise
Mansions, riches, surfeits and rewards,
Which they will never know or dream of
Because their tired, worn-out limbs
Can only carry them from their chained labour
To the final sleep and comfort of the Earth.

The poet's task is to speak for the oppressed
And to remove the spear from Christ's side,
For Christ cries out for all men
Who feed on His flesh till none is left;
He cries for all — black, yellow or white —
Who cyclically have their brains blown out
By mines, shells, bullets or bombs,
To conform with the earth's primal law
Of testing basic truths in human blood,
And all these men die in sorrow
At the futility and lies which destroy their lives.

FLORENCE
Ara vos prec, per aquella valor
que vos guida al som de l'escalina.

Tall house, steep stairs
And, all around, the Tuscan hills
Brooding over a simmering urn
In which God has brewed more genius
Than in any other city on earth.
No flat land, except the narrow bed
Of the Arno; every lane leads up or down,
Down to Hell, or up to Purgatory and Heaven.

Day in and day out, for thirty years
Or more, like an eagle entangled in his wings,
He hopped from the cobbled street
Through a narrow door on an escalina
With a banister rope, up to his nest,
Where, master of thunder and lightning,
He wove on the loom of his mind a cloth
Which no human hand could unravel.

From the dizzy heights of his flight
He peered down circle upon circle,
Into the dark of Hell where friends
And foes crawled and writhed in pain.

Then, one day, he rose along the slopes
Of the mountain of Purgatory — the Apennines,
Which overlook his beloved Florence —
And from there, higher, or lower,
According to the elements in which he moved:
To the plains of Ravenna, or to the Empyrean
Of Paradise, gazed at from exile
By a lonely eagle circling the hills,
Lured higher and higher by the dream
Of the fairest woman, more than woman,

Mostly gold, no loam, except in name,
Fused in the crucible of his mind
Into the music which can lift
Human dust to the threshold of light.

And all the time, whether in his house
With the purgatorial, narrow stairs,
Or by his tomb where his unquiet bones,
Once shuffled from place to place to avoid
The predatory hands of those who compelled him
To eat the bitter bread of exile,
Now rest at last
By the wall of a Franciscan monastery,
I thought of another great soul,
A devoted friend of his, friend of mine too,
Much obsessed by stairs, purgatorial climbs,
Pentecostal fires and Paradise glimpsed
Through suffering, shedding of hopes
And desires, and the nakedness of the heart.
By the marble wall where Dante's remains
Burn like radium and illumine all around,
I ceaselessly thought of a granite wall
In the leafy world of an English shire
Where lie the ashes of a modern Dante.

EDINBURGH

History-drenched city, full of dreams,
Caught in the grey stones of streets,
From castle, cathedral and palace
To Georgian houses, Adam squares
And Doric columns of a Nordic Parthenon.

Cobbled lanes ringing with hallowed names,
Twisting wynds, narrow vaults
Through which History mused, and watched
The intricate dance of Love and Death.

Latticed windows through which a prophet
Cast frustrated glances and curses
On a palace where a Queen moved in a maze
Of ploys which led to her death.

Oh, to gaze at the ghost-haunted walls
Of the castle, caught in a blue haze
Of floating clouds, or falling night,
To measure the hours by the needle
Of Scott's monument, in Princes Street,
Or the minutes by the clip-clop of fountains
From bronze nymphs in its green gardens
Spelling out history in watery sunlight,
To meet again a world where spent years
Have left furrows in the heart
And no traces on the dumb granite!

A CROW AND I

A crow and I, side by side,
Head askew in the slanting sun,
Hobble along on a golf-course,
Each thinking his own separate thoughts.

He is listening for, seeing everywhere
The hooded worm which will feed him,
Which has fed on my ancestral selves
And will some day feed on my cells.

So the crow eats me who eat him
Through mould, plants and animals,
Continuous transformation, snake biting its tail,
Image of Earth's self-devouring cycle.

What is the meaning of it all?
The crow does not ask such questions,
Man ceaselessly does, for he knows
That everything that lives must die,

That birth and death on indifferent earth
Begin and end with the same moan,
That to love and die point to the truth
That the womb and the grave are one.

A TREE

A tree points its five bare fingers
To the sky, clawing at passing clouds,
Calling to God to be lifted out of the earth
To the freedom of flying, falling leaves.

— Oh God, stretch out your burning arms
Towards me, and cleave me to the ground,
So that from your blinding light
And my dust, new births may come!

Sick to the roots, half dead,
Dazzled and tormented by not seeing,
I watch my seedlings wilt in my shade;
Oh, let me die so that they may live!

In hospitals, in sick rooms,
Aching, heart-broken human beings
Long for death, to free their loved ones
From the harrowing weight of their own suffering.

HOW CAN I?

Oh God, how can I understand
This continuous reduction
Of myself, this slow death in life,
Until the heart finally stops?

How can I accept the sealed box
Which will take me down
Into the depth of the earth and float
Me through the dark waters of silence?

How can I accept the closing down
Of the senses, the whitening of the mind,
The eyes and ears turned to stones
And rolled to and fro by dying seas?

How can I go on living, hoping
That the battered heart will not falter
In fear, and give up its Sisyphus' task
Of ceaselessly pulsing on its red flood?

TIME

Time's black waters roll
On, gnawing us cell after cell,
Young and old, rich and poor,
With loving or treacherous heart,
To the fecund depth of the ocean
From where life will rise again
In translucent algae and plankton.

Like a dying star, man
Ceaselessly rises
Across the changing sky and falls
Into the living abyss of the night.
Only the distant sound of a name
And the luminous shape of a loved face
Can bring to him the strength
To face the unknown.

ECLIPSE

The moon has eaten up a large chunk
Of the sun,
Grief has eaten up a large part
Of the heart.
What remains?
— A flickering candle-light to decipher
A few lines scribbled on a page,
A diminished, tired body to go round
A few more days and nights
Till the final eclipse,
When sun and moon, life and death,
Are one.

CONVERSATION

Caught in a trap, half-frozen,
Black upon white, a crow curses
Man's cruelty for denying him
A seed or a root to survive the winter snow;

Wings spread out, head bent,
One leg half cut by steel,
He struggles in vain to overcome fate
And to avoid the executioner's hand.

Ashamed by his fear, ashamed for man,
Half numb in the November wind
Sweeping westward on a Scottish hill,
I fumble in haste for my penknife.

Bracing himself up for the last stand
Of the losing game, beak wide open
To the four winds of cursed earth,
He lets out a final, defiant cry.

Knife in hand, I bend towards him,
Humbly apologizing for the evil done
To a black, age-old friend
Whom God holds with me in His hand.

He suddenly understands that the same blood
Runs in our veins, and that the same kiln
Has baked and cast into the world
These two products of the same potter's hand,

And with the round diamond of his eyes
Beamed upon me like distant stars,
Wings in repose, one leg folded,
The other outstretched, he waits;

I come closer, and with a swift stroke
I cut the white tendon caught
In steel teeth, and black-cloaked,
One-legged John Silver hops on a nearby tree.

We look at each other in silence,
Reconciled in the hand of our Maker
Who watches aghast and helpless
The sickness which eats up his children.

A worm or a fly blindly kills a lion,
Man alone, most cruel of all
Animals, wilfully kills against reason,
Unaware of the disease which gnaws his soul,

For, if worms, lions or flies
Can only die the moment of their death,
Man, who dies and knows it, dies
From the very moment of his birth.

A VOICE

A voice sweeps me over the clouds
Of years, back to dazzling sun
And dancing shadows in olive groves,
Where light stands still at noon
Over wilting leaves and cicada songs.

A million years divide me from this world,
And, across the rocky chasm of the mind
Crater-pocked by Time's meteorites
Caught upon the retina of an aged eye,
Surge the intricate figures of a dance,
Which soon turns into a funeral march,
Along a rocky coast, by the blue sea,
Where the millennial shapes which I have used,
And will use again, in other climes,
Whatever my name or place of rebirth,
Will remember the music of the primal dream.

There are those who see the brain
As a complex telephone exchange or a computer —
Equation of matter — destined to be dissolved
Wholly and absolutely into eternal dust,
They forget the fact that the human brain
Is only the rope of a millenary-old kite,
Hauled across the earth and the stars,
Retaining, according to its means, visions
Of Adam, of his songs, and receding quasars,
Something which cannot be reduced to a cranium-
Box, or measured by encephalograms.

I am neither Plato by the Ionian Sea
Nor Augustine by the salt-soaked African sands,
Yet their voices still linger in the continuum of space,
And the puny, computer-like instrument

Called the brain can sometimes catch echoes
Of them, and thus inspire men with the hope
That once feet and eyes return to earth,
The brain, which guided them
To the meeting point of what has been
And will be, will retain visions
To be reborn over and over again,
In other cells, until Time's end
And the dissolving of the earth
Into the essential gauze which enfolds
The first living molecule and the eternal whole.

EVE

A naked woman saved a city,
A woman in armour saved a nation,
Another, newly-born, under the apple tree
Lured Adam into the joy of creation.

Was it the light in the apple leaves,
The voice of the wind in the oak trees
Or the strange whispers in the spring air,
That inspired these single-minded Eves?

Who knows? Woman's roots run deep
Down to the living dark of the sea
Into the silent womb of primal clay
Where lies the seed of the apple tree.

MEDITERRANEAN EVENING

Criss-crossing of telephone wires,
The sun slides on them, bright
Ball, towards a pole marking the hours
On a dial of mimosa trees and blue clouds.

A procession of green-clad, white-coiffed
Daffodils sidles along a wall
Towards a small, chapel-like
Cottage, for the evensong of twittering birds.

Streams of water shimmer in the sun,
Fast flowing towards dark holes
And silence. What remains
Of light and water, of sun and dreams?

Where have they gone, all those
Whose minds and hearts have echoed
With ours, where are the visions,
The sighs and joys which made their lives?

Can they all have died with the breath
Which caused the rises and falls
Of their lungs and kept their hearts
And bodies tied to the rolling wheel?

Can spirit only live, only survive
When molecules of matter are fused
Into a body, an animal or a tree,
Or has spirit its own mysterious universe?

Who knows? I believe that there is a darkness
Which human sight cannot pierce,
That there are lights and sounds which eyes
Or ears cannot hear or descry,

I believe that the world of spirit, uncharted
By man, is not composed of isolated fragments,
But is a whole in which every individual being
Is part of a timeless, all-embracing Being.

This, of course, no man can prove,
And though the conscious mind may strive
To unveil the truth on the other side of the grave,
No light can match that of vision or dream.

THE SEA

Uncoiled silver under the revolving stars,
Golden whirls in the noonday sun,
Spray-born vestal pouring praise
At the feet of rocks at evensong,
Or passion and rage under changing veils,
Hair loosened over their shoulders,
Invading every crevice, covering in foam
Every spur, until she falls back, spent,
Unlocked in tidal sleep,
To begin again the age-long love scene
Between rock and sea, which will only end
On stilled shores where all music is one.

Woman — sea, life-giving water,
Flooding estuaries and promontories
With the ecstasy of the primal dawn,
Whispering music no voice can sing,
Infinite bosom, tomb,
Upon which man, cleansed
From his bitter years, finds
His last rest among the stars
Which silently weave the dust
From which rose woman and sea.

TODAY

Today the wind in the oak trees
Caught me in a whirl of leaves
And floated me back many years ago,
Flat on my back on a mountain slope,
Lulled by the music of pine needles,
Watching clouds scurrying in the sky.

Now, twenty-two years have passed,
Many summers, and even more winters,
And I listen again to the wind in the leaves
Of trees on the slopes of an English hill.

The world has turned round many times
And it shows a very different face.
No lofty rocks or secluded vales
Robed in the stiff glory of dark green,
No dancing clouds by mountain tops,
No eagles or hawks hovering above,
Cyclically breaking the monotony of the wind
With their haunting, melancholy cry.

We were then lying on our backs,
Stunned by the heat of summer noon,
We were young overflowing with hopes,
Unlived joys and the gleaming lights
Of wide open, undimmed eyes;
It was your first visit to a land .
Which, since young, you had often dreamt of.

Now, you are no longer here, or there,
But a suspended form, asleep in the earth,
A living soul, an eye, a voice,
Continuous part of light and darkness.
My mind, swept by sad perplexities
While I stand here cut from senses, relives
These faded hours and past joys,

And achingly wonders where now they are
And why in a world of recurring abundance
We are allowed so little from the riches
Of a universe which measures its own existence
By an undefined span of light years,
While ours is only a gasp between birth and death.

What are the differences that tell
On the uncharted loom of the Eternal?
Not those measured by human hearts and minds,
For they can only be infinitesimally small
And inaudible in the unplumbed silence;
Only the incandescent moments lived
On the wings of flights beyond good and evil,
And the belief, not that we must love
One another or die, but that we must
Love one another because we die,
Can lift man to eternal truth.

SUN

A sudden shudder, and the hallowed head surges
From the sea, spilling gold over her limbs
Stretched out at my feet long, long ago,
Back to the dawn of the world
When the first human eye, free from loam,
Caught the first rays of light, whose
Golden dust still lingers around.

The sun slowly rolls across the sky,
Shrinks all shapes to a sheet of light,
Till suddenly all landmarks and masses merge
Into the blue, dewy light of coming night,
And with the moon taking up watch on a cloud,
He lays his head to rest on a hill,
To be lulled to sleep by the rises and falls
And the infinite murmur of the sea.

CANNES – EVENING

A cacophony of birds fills the plane trees
Of the avenue, streaked with luminous swords
Criss-crossing one another in endless flashes
Midst the dying roar of the city and the sea.

A sudden silence, the presence of a woman
With eyes like the setting sun.
Scything seas strewn with wild sails,
Some hastening to the safety of harbours,
Others adrift in the depths of waves
Where float unanchored hulls.

Turnerian colours, light and shades,
Dream islands, bottomless abysses
Flow endlessly past the vision
Overcast with passing shadows
Which no smile can dispel.

Wandering soul looking for your haven,
Will you ever find it? Perhaps, perhaps not;
Whatever happens, the stars that watch
Over you will bring to you the dream
Which the earth will have denied you.

SETTING SUN

Golden sun, fountain of fire
Rising from the depth of the sea,
Woman – blue wave,
Meteor, trailing behind the light
Which brings dazzling sight
And the terrors
Of the ensuing night.

MOUNTAIN LAKES

Golden lakes, fringed with shadows,
Carved out by God's first gaze
From the shoulders of mountains,
Reflecting millenary sails,
Sunken cities, submerged temples,
Lost worlds, dishevelled weeds,
Mirrors — memories of the world's soul,
In which the sky weaves for the earth
The golden loom of the eternal light.

PRESENCE

Presence is haunted by absence,
You are all there in front of me,
And by being so, you summon all
That is not there and will never be,
You are a flower in a desert
Which I shall never cross,
I can smell its scent, but the touch
Of its petals is forever out of reach,
You have all the riches of summer
About you, but behind them lurks the frost
And desolation of barren winter,
You are both wealth and poverty,
Radiating, life-giving warmth
And the cold of the grave, all in one,
So that to see you is to be hollowed
By what is missing and to know
That you are what you are not,
And that I, caught between the two,
Am like embers, neither alive nor dead,
In the tidal winds of absence and presence.

WOMAN ASLEEP

Daughter of the sun fallen upon the earth,
Clad in rocks and green valleys,
Sigh from Heaven, millenary bosom,
Breath melting away the bitterness of life,
Bed of flowers upon which to float
To ecstatic worlds; cloudless roof,
Marine statue carved upon the sand
By the blue eternity of the indifferent sea,
Music echoing memories of the dark,
Tomb trembling under the weight of dreams,
Days and nights rhythmed by the changing gaze
Of the sun, pouring down showers of stars
Which turn all flowers into haunting eyes.

ABSENCE

Absence reduces me to silence,
I cannot make you with words,
Or replace you by words;
Like God, or primal man,
I make with my hands
And shape thoughts and feelings
On the turbulence of the wind;
I mould your fluid body
On the changing volutes of the leaves,
Carve your face on the dark of night
Or draw it on the bark of trees,
Tables, walls and other surfaces,
I draw your hair, your eyes,
Your smile — circle of light,
And at the end of it all
I am left with an image,
A translucence on the wall of the brain,
Which is less than you are
And more than I shall ever hold.

WOMAN FROM A PAINTING

Surged from the mysterious world
Of Lenain, La Tour, Vermeer,
Striding across Northern plains —
Windswept, water-laced —
White-coiffed, flashing wings,
Seagulls moving to distant horizons
Where earth and sky blend
Into grey, swaying haze
Full of sounds past, present
And future, reflecting their meaning
On a face, risen from the sea,
Pursuing throughout the centuries
And the fire and mire of life,
Glimmers of the undying light
And the dark from which life was made.

I REMEMBER

I remember yesterday, I remember tomorrow,
The day after tomorrow, and all tomorrows
To come, but I can never remember today,
Because there is no today; it is always yesterday
Or tomorrow, I have been, or I shall be,
But never I am, for I have no present,
I am only the meeting point of two currents —
One which has been, and another that will be.

I am an absence, which makes from what has been
A greater, richer and all-embracing presence,
Which, like a seed, first sown in a pot,
Grows and spreads to fill a whole garden,

I say: ' I am', yet this 'I am' is a nothingness
Which can only be if absence becomes presence,
If yesterday and tomorrow become one,
Without any present which is a negation of both.

IF ONE DAY

If one day,
Uncertain of your fate,
You came to forget
What I did once say
To you,
Or the traces
I have left
On the inner dark
Of your mind,
Do not look for guidance
In the wrinkles of your face
Or in the changing colour
Of your hair,
Only remember the sign
Which, beyond bitter seas
And the bruises of the earth,
Will lead your winged spirit
To the isle of eternal rest.

MEMENTO YEATS

I know all too well why Yeats
Raged at the absurdity of age;
What's more trying than a heart and mind
Wanting to leap over waterfalls,
Climb mountains, discover new lands,
Finding that the tired body refuses to obey?
What's more galling than to dream
Of past summers and journeys done,
Of silken hair and golden arms,
Of smiles and eyes won or lost,
And to realise that it only remains
To sit and watch the meanderings of the mind
While the heart, whether it likes it or not,
Has to reconcile itself to the coming cold?

Yet, the sun's rays are never warmer
Than when their source is about to disappear.
The aged body falters, the heart
Never grows old or alters, until it stops;
Neither young nor old, it goes on
Quickening the pulse, feeding dreams,
Pouring out songs, irrespective of seasons.

Though the sap may rise slower
In the boughs, birds continue their music,
Unaware of coming frost or winter,
Entirely lost in the joy of their task;
Man's autumn-song — a symphony
Of sorrows — russet leaves
From a bare, broken tree,
Is always shot through with sadness
And the awareness of the impending dark.

MORNING

Slowly, your face rises from its dream of night,
Your eyes, pure as mountain snow
Or angels' tears, unseal upon a world
In which we all breathe the same air
And wonder why the wide-eyed sun pours
With indifference its light and warmth
On those who sleep sound or breathe as one
And on those whom a strange, incomprehensible fate
Has ground under sorrows, or torn apart.

Yet, on reflection, there is no cause for wonder,
For, unless the grain dies, there is no wheat,
Olives and grapes must be ground or squeezed
So that they may yield their fruit;
All that lives must ache or dream of substance
While clasping shadows, or lying on a cross;
There is neither life nor love without tears.

WISDOM IS WAITING

Do not ask for the golden fleece,
For Helen's smile or enfolding arms;
Remember Orpheus, do not turn,
Do not move before it's time,

Listen for the song from the oak tree,
Try to catch the murmur of the earth,
Or be lulled to sleep on the bosom of the sea,
But never try to grasp what is not ripe,

Sit on the banks of the river and wait
For Melusine to come and shed her skirt
And jewels, but unless you have one eye
In the forehead, you'll never see her,

Tristram never wooed or pursued Iseult
They just met, and recognised each other,
Buddha and Christ never sought wisdom,
They waited, under a tree, or in the desert,

Your heart may break at the thought
Of eyes, lips or a shape you long to hold,
But forced love never grows, waited words
Never come, a watched clock hardly moves,

So, cultivate patience, expect nothing,
Love and grace unfold at their own pace,
Forsake St. Vitus' dance and the dream
Of action; remember that wisdom is waiting.

PENELOPE – SEA

Who is the Odysseus the Sea is waiting for,
Where is he, when will he come home
To his Penelope-Sea, weaving and unweaving,
Night and day, not for a score of years,
But for aeons of years past and to come,
A web of waves, of foam and spray
That puts all human art to shame
And fills the mind with dismay?

If a mere mortal could, for so many years,
Drive back and forth the shuttle
Which wove and unwove the plot
Of silver and gold thread which kept
Her suitors at bay, waiting for the return
Of her true love, what longings, what dreams
Must haunt and restlessly heave the bosom
Of the sea towards her wandering Odysseus!

Is this Odysseus, Adam unparadised,
Torn away from Eve's enfolding arms?
Is the Penelope-Sea fallen Eve,
Cause of the earth's and Adam's fall
From God's undivided bosom and Heaven?
Perhaps, for it is from the Sea-Eve
That life and the earth's progeny arose
And will go on spreading, fighting and dying
Until, at last, barren, exhausted Earth
Sleeps in peace in the Sea's barren arms.

WHY SHOULD YOU?

Why should you be upset by the thought
That it might have been better if you
And I had never met, or if you had never left
Your quiet coves and different skies?

True, you would have been spared troubled nights,
Insomniac hours between evening and dawn,
And attempts to remake with crumbs and illusions
The longed-for oneness which fate has torn apart.

You might have been different! You might!
But that would not have been you, with a mind
Taut like a sail in the wind, and a heart
Ready to rise like a bird on the wing.

Entombed in its body, tense under its veil,
Your soul, questing for the strange music,
Which no master can make, could only be still,
Once it had consumed itself for music's sake.

Now, face to face with yourself, staring on air,
Clutching imaginary nothings in your arms,
Heaping impossibilities upon might-have-beens,
You seek in vain in sleep the likeness of dreams.

You wonder, in the broken world in which you live,
If this trial by music was really necessary,
So as to unlace the springs of your heart, and marry
In you song and sigh, joy and grief.

Take a crystal glass, full of pure water,
Look at the light, look at the sun through it,
You cannot tell whether it's full or empty,
You can only turn away from it, in despair.

Only a gesture, or an all-seeing eye, could point
The difference between the two, only a wound
Can decide whether or not you have a heart,
Only love can tell whether or not you can love.

What you might have been cannot be known,
Since it is not, and has never been.
All you do is to project imaginary dreams in space,
And you are space hallowed by imagination.

VIOLETS AND POPPIES

There was a time when I saw more poppies
Than violets, a time when the road ran upward,
And I was in a hurry to reach the top
Of the hill, eager to discover new worlds.

Now the road lies downwards, on a slope
Which knows no rises, no wonder cities,
No restful plains or enticing discoveries,
Except the mystery of the end and final sleep.

So, I take time and walk with care
Along woods and shores shot with gleams
Of setting light, and sometimes pause and stare
At unexpected glimpses of lost dreams.

I recognize them, but can do no more
Than a mother who wrings her hands in despair
At the sight of her child swept away
By tempest-tossed waves or torrential waters.

They have gone from me, and casual time
Never keeps account of wasted hours
Or missed chances, for, as Heraclitus said,
We never dip our feet twice in the same river.

The water moves, time moves, or we move,
Faster and faster, and the chill evening air
Reminds us to hurry over things undone
And to gather fast the things we care,

Yet the things we care cannot be gathered
Or taken with us, and we leave this earth
Empty-handed, with gestures unmade, haunted
By thoughts and words cut off from breath.

The heart never ceases to ache until it breaks,
It sustains life and endures loss;
Anxiety and joy, light and darkness
Rise and fall with its unpredictable beats.

DAWN

Darkness frays, whitens,
The day struggles to be born;
Floating shapes coalesce
And compose their masses,
Amber coils slip through the shutters,
Lassoing fleeting shadows
On skin-coloured sands,
The day rises with a golden tide
In which I move and dive
To depths where I find myself,
And know myself through a being
Streaming with the dew of primal dawn
In a world of shadows,
Where everything is true —
Music without instruments,
Flowers without stems or roots
Dancing in azurean meadows.

SEA AND EARTH

Systole and diastole, ebb and flow,
Rise and fall of sea on sand,
Sea — womb and grave of life,
Solid flesh and liquid loam
Caught in a dialogue as long as Time.

What weight, what place does man
Occupy in this mythical marriage
Of two forces which give him life?
Much less than that of a grain of sand
On the slope of mountains or on the moon.

That is to say none: he comes,
And will go, unnoticed by earth or sea,
And neither will miss a breath
Or record a sigh of sorrow
On the night of his final death.

Protests or curses are equally vain,
All he can do is to accept his fate —
To be born and to die in pain,
To be tossed between fears and joys,
To dream of love and live in sorrows,
To move around with stars in his head
And never to forget his final bed,
To endure with equal patience the love
That transforms and that which tears apart;
Above all to learn from the dawn of life
To familiarise himself with the thought
That each beat of his heart might be the last,
And to think that, whatever happens,
All is well in this world and in the next.

SCOTLAND
To J.P.

The vague sense of having been here
Before, haunted my young days and led
Me to this land in pursuit of dreams
Which, whatever reality they gained,
Always left something to be discovered.

Wherever I may be, in sunny Provence
Or misty London, I see Scottish hills,
A Highland burn roaring down rippling falls,
Landing in a dark, peat-coated pool;
Then, after twists and turns, froth and foam,
It tears itself away from Death's embrace
To plunge headlong towards home —
The sea — and, waving its white bonnet
And plumes to rowan trees, it slips
Past the stony legs of a humpbacked bridge,
And promontories of dew-laden moor,
Through green hollows and ferny braes,
To finally fade away into a shawl of heather.

I see fairies dancing on the Eildon Hills,
And dark-eyed lochs asleep in the lap
Of green-fringed slopes or moors wrapped
In silence only broken by the curlew's cry.

Katrine, Lomond, Mallaig, Lubnaig,
The Tay, the Tweed! These names
Are always music to my ears, and laughter and tears
In Edinburgh's High Street or Holyrood Palace
Call forth memories as old as the seas.

LIGHT

Awake or asleep, we cannot know
Whether we live or dream;
Only in the night of death
Will we find a light
Lighter than any light,
Free from any shadows,
From yesterdays and tomorrows,
Eternal, ever the same,
A transparency of Being
Unstained by anything human,
Held in infinite suspense
By the music of the universe.

CLOUDS

A host of clouds
Harried by the wind
Streaks across the sky
Like a herd of wild horses
In a Western;
Their mass frays
At the edges, breaks,
Feathers into fragments,
Lassoed
By the white dust
Or the blue,
Which swiftly swamps them
And dissolves them
Into nothing.

QUESTIONS

A crow, scuffling in a hedge,
Stretches one wing, then the other,
To show me — his doctor —
How badly arthrosis affects him.

What can I do for him?
Nothing; neither can he for me.

We look at each other
Under an indifferent sky
Streaked with fleeing clouds
Unfolding over hills and tree tops
A turbulence of forms,
Intimations of being,
Through which the ebb and flow
Of life, today and tomorrow
Shimmer, and leave the mind
Helpless in the face
Of so much loveliness
And so little solace.

LIKE MUSIC

Like music
You move everywhere,
Invade everything;
You dissolve yourself
And flow in my veins,
You lend golden lips
To laughter
And solar rays
To the eyes;

You rise and water spills
Diamonds in your wake,
You move and trees follow;
You join mountains and plains,
Earth and sky,
Fire and ice,
Darkness and light.
You are everywhere, and nowhere,
You are the light upon the sea,
The wave whispering to the shore
The lullaby of Eternity.

WHO AM I?

Where am I, who am I?
For Plato, I am only spume
On the shores of Eternity; for Berkeley
The world lives in my eye.

Perhaps it does, but how do I
Know the real from the dream,
How do I separate percepts
From their transcriptions by mind?

Where does the task of the one end,
Where does that of the other begin?
— Idle thoughts, waste of time,
Nothing in life has beginning or end;

It's all continuations, translucencies
Of Being, metaphors of light,
Complex patterns of dissemblances,
Will o' the wisps between dawn and twilight.

KEW GARDENS 1974

The stern-faced keeper hobbles past
Three companies of tulips
Standing on guard, their yellow-plumed
Helmets swaying in the breeze.

A black-capped field-marshal duck
Wobbles along, his round eye —
Gold-circled diamond — swivels by
Green stalks transfixed in its stare.

The sun spills silver
On a glass dome which burns
White in a kaleidoscope of colours —
The tree of knowledge
Glimmers under ice.

I sit on a bench,
Still as water in a pond,
A ghost, my mind lost
In space, or out of it.

Shadows flit across
The screen of my eyes —
Boundless oceans
In which the mind descries
The content of its dreams.

Time passes, unrecorded,
Unaccounted for, until a hand
Brings the mind back to earth,
And I find myself at the gate
At falling night.

HOSPITAL

A bunch of rose buds —
Girls in their teens —
Bring light and spring
Into the desolation
Of the hospital room.

By the following morning,
The heat of one single night
Has turned them
Into full-blown women
Attuned to the desolation
Of the hospital room.

The nurse comes in,
Pulls the curtains,
Drops a "good morning"
Mechanical as cold tea,
And walks breezily out,
Leaving the door open.

Clatter of pans and tea cups,
A bed is wheeled by,
Someone is going down;
What will be the result?
— Home for a brief spell,
Or the end of broken sleep!

Day and night,
In every room or ward,
With piped music
And propitiatory flowers
On bedside tables, men
And women anxiously wonder
When they will leave,
Or return here,
For the last time.

MAN

God's dream through time,
Caught like a moth
In a shaft of light, man
Longs for the lost Eden
And the last turn of the wheel.

When God finally awakens
And opens His eye,
Its burning rays
Will destroy all shadows,
Dispel all dreams,
And nothing will remain
But a lidless eye, lost
In the glare of its light.

MORNING WALK

I walk through the amber and gold
Of dew-laden irises and jonquils;
Around me, sea-gulls fill
The air with their screeches and squabbles,
And ceaselessly unfold a whole euclidian
Geometry in the sky; their will
Is their greed for food and space,
And they plummet down like stones
Or rise and fall in infinite circles.

A sudden wind whips the sea —
Waves, pouring their white lace
On the shore where I stand lost in dreams
Of worlds, golden, still unborn.
Far away, in the distance, on a headland
Cyclically wrapped in explosions of spray,
Odysseus, stone statue on his rock,
Calmly gazes at the serpent-roll
Of the waves, and pours around him
The age-long tide of his wisdom
Which will only find its final rest
On Death's life-giving bosom.

LIBRARY OF DAVIDSON COLLEGE

Books on regular loan may be checked out for **two weeks**. Books must be presented at the Circulation Desk in or...

fter d...

... of